Welcome to the

Handbook

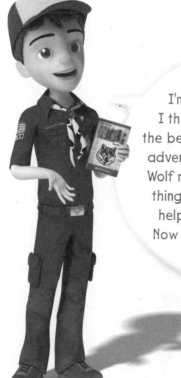

Hi! My name is Ethan. I'm a Bear this year, and I think being a Cub Scout is the best. I'm going to be in each adventure as you work on your Wolf rank. I'll tell you about fun things I did as a Wolf, and I'll help you out along the way. Now turn the page, and start the Wolf adventure!

33450
ISBN 978-0-8395-0040-7
© 2015 Boy Scouts of America
2015 Printing

Table of Contents

WOLF REQUIRED ADVENTURES

WOLF ELECTIVE ADVENTURES

Wolf Parent Introduction

If you could give only one gift to your son, what would it be? No matter what your family situation, it is within your power to help him grow into a person with a good feeling about himself and a genuine concern for others. Cub Scouting can assist you in providing this greatest gift of all.

Today your son is a Wolf, but soon he will graduate into a Bear den. Later, he'll work to achieve the Webelos and Arrow of Light ranks. This will prepare him for more adventure as a Boy Scout and the opportunity to earn Scouting's highest rank—Eagle Scout.

Using This Handbook

This handbook is written for both you and your Wolf. Much of it is for your son to enjoy, while other sections like this parent information are for you as an adult. However, it is our hope that you will read the adventures along with your Wolf and help him to achieve them!

Your Son, Scouting, and You

As a parent or other caring adult, you want your Wolf to grow up to be self-reliant and dependable, worthy and caring. Scouting has these same goals in mind for him.

The mission of the Boy Scouts of America is to prepare young people to make ethical and moral choices over their lifetimes by instilling in them the values of the Scout Oath and Scout Law.

Scout Oath (or Promise)	Scout Law
On my honor I will do my best To do my duty to God and my country and to obey the Scout Law; To help other people at all times; To keep myself physically strong, mentally awake, and morally straight.	A Scout is trustworthy, loyal, helpful, friendly, courteous, kind, obedient, cheerful, thrifty, brave, clean, and reverent.

The Scout Oath and the Scout Law are defined on pages 18 through 21 in the Bobcat requirements.

Since 1910, the Boy Scouts of America has been weaving lifetime values into fun, developmental activities. These activities are designed to help families teach their sons how to make good decisions throughout their lives and give them confidence as they become the adult leaders of tomorrow.

In a society where your son is often taught that winning is everything, Cub Scouting teaches him to DO HIS BEST, to help others, and to try to live his life according to the Scout Oath and the Scout Law. If a Cub Scout has done his best to satisfy a requirement, then he has met the standard for advancement in Cub Scouts. It is up to his parent and den leader to gauge whether he has offered his best effort.

The Purposes of Cub Scouting

Cub Scouting is a year-round family-oriented part of the BSA program designed for boys who are in first through fifth grades (or are 7, 8, 9, and 10 years old). Parents, leaders, and organizations work together to achieve the Purposes of Cub Scouting.

1. Character Development
2. Spiritual Growth
3. Good Citizenship
4. Sportsmanship and Fitness
5. Family Understanding
6. Respectful Relationships
7. Personal Achievement
8. Friendly Service
9. Fun and Adventure
10. Preparation for Boy Scouts

Cub Scout Den

Your Cub Scout is a member of a den. The Wolf den will involve your son in a group of boys his own age where he can earn recognition for his accomplishments. He will also gain a sense of personal achievement from the skills he learns. Most dens have six to eight boys and meet two to three times a month. Den meetings are a time for learning new things, having fun, and going on outings. Dens are led by a team of adult volunteers—the den leader and assistant den leader(s).

Cub Scout Pack Leadership

Your Wolf is also a member of a Cub Scout pack. Most packs are made up of several dens that gather monthly at a pack meeting. The meeting usually follows a suggested theme, and it's a time for boys to be recognized for their accomplishments during the month, to perform skits and songs they have learned in den meetings, and to have fun with the entire family.

Packs are led by a Cubmaster and pack committee. Like the den leaders, the Cubmaster and assistants are volunteer leaders—usually family members of boys in the pack. The pack committee makes plans for pack meetings and activities and takes care of the "business" items that are necessary for a pack to operate smoothly.

Each pack is sponsored by a chartered organization. This is a community organization that has applied for and received a charter from the Boy Scouts of America National Council to operate the Scouting program. The chartered organization may be a school, service club, religious group, or other group interested in youth. The chartered organization sponsors the pack, approves the leadership of the pack, provides a meeting place, and operates the pack within the guidelines and policies of that organization and the Boy Scouts of America.

Your Wolf's Advancement

In Scouting, advancement is the process by which a member meets certain requirements and earns recognition. The Wolf advancement program is a blend of activities that boys complete in their den meetings as well as at home with their families.

If your son is a new Cub Scout, the first step in the advancement process is to earn the Bobcat badge (see page 16). The Bobcat requirements serve to orient a new Scout to the ideals and symbols of Scouting. When all of the Bobcat requirements have been completed, your boy becomes eligible to receive his Bobcat badge in a pack ceremony.

As a Wolf, your son will work toward earning the Wolf rank. This rank is for those boys who are in the second grade or are 8 years old. All the Cub Scout ranks (Tiger, Wolf, Bear, Webelos, and Arrow of Light) are tailored for a grade and the corresponding age level. To advance, Wolves work on the adventures described in this handbook, some required and some elective.

As your son completes each requirement in an adventure to the best of his ability, you or another caring adult will sign the space marked "Akela's OK." His den leader will sign where it says, "Den Leader's OK." If the requirement is completed in a den meeting, the den leader may sign both places.

| Akela's OK | Date | Den Leader's OK |

Akela means "good leader" and is an important part of Cub Scouting. Akela can be you, a den leader, a teacher, or another important adult. Scouts can track their requirements in the Wolf Adventure Tracking section found at the back of the book. As boys advance, they earn adventure loops and pins to mark their progress. These items will be presented to them during a ceremony at a pack or den meeting. It is important for boys to be recognized for the good work they do!

Do Your Best

Your Wolf can keep track of his adventures using the Wolf Adventure Tracking on page 309 of this handbook. This provides encouragement and helps him see his progress toward the Wolf rank. Whenever possible, adventure requirements are written in a way that allows them to be customized for each boy and den. Boys are never "tested" or placed in a position where they may not be successful. If a Cub Scout has participated and done his best to satisfy a requirement, then he has met the standard for advancement in Cub Scouts. It is up to his parent and den leader to gauge whether he has offered his best effort.

If a Wolf is unable to participate in a den or pack activity due to an illness or conflict, you may work with him to complete the requirements to the best of his ability, but please make every effort to help him attend each meeting so he can get the full benefit of the Cub Scouting program.

If your Wolf has an intellectual or physical disability that prevents him from attempting a requirement, talk to your den leader and Cubmaster about finding an alternative.

Wolf Badge

The Wolf badge is awarded when boys have completed the following:

1. Complete each of the following Wolf required adventures with your den or family:

Required Adventures		
Call of the Wild	Council Fire	Duty to God Footsteps
Howling at the Moon	Paws on the Path	Running With the Pack

2. Complete one Wolf elective adventure of your den or family's choosing.

3. With your parent or guardian, complete the exercises in the pamphlet *How to Protect Your Children From Child Abuse: A Parent's Guide*, and earn the Cyber Chip award for your age.*

*If your family does not have Internet access at home AND you do not have ready Internet access at school or another public place or via a mobile device, the Cyber Chip portion of this requirement may be waived by your parent or guardian.

Family participation is an integral part of the advancement process, and there are many chances to join in activities that are age-appropriate for your child. You may sign the "Akela's OK" in his handbook each time he finishes a requirement, and you should always notify the den leader when a requirement is completed at home.

The Wolf badge is presented during a special ceremony at a pack meeting to each boy's parent or guardian, who in turn presents it to the Scout. The badge is worn on the left uniform pocket. (See page 12 or inside the back cover.)

Scouting and Duty to God

The Boy Scouts of America has always held steadfastly to the principle, embodied in the Scout Oath, that a Scout has a duty to God. The BSA does not promote any specific religion, and has always embraced all faiths. We do encourage youth members and their families to be active in their own faith, in keeping with the BSA's Declaration of Religious Principle.

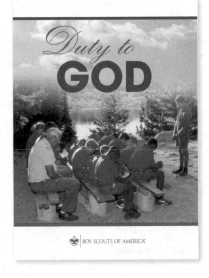

It naturally follows that the leadership for your son's spiritual development, both within and outside Cub Scouting, must come primarily from your home and your family's religious leaders. Your son will look to you as his example of how to learn and perform his duty to God.

The adventures related to duty to God in each rank of the Cub Scouting program provide support, and each boy has the opportunity to earn the religious emblem of his faith. The emblem is created and presented by your son's religious group. Most of the world's religions have an emblem of their faith. However, alternative requirements are available for boys whose faith institutions do not have an emblem or whose families are not affiliated with an organized religious group.

In addition, the staff at your BSA local council service center should be able to help. Many local councils and districts offer organized opportunities for Scouts to earn their religious emblems while meeting and sharing fellowship with other Scouts of their faith.

 You can also find information on the Internet at **www.praypub.org** or **www.scouting.org/filestore/pdf/512-879_WB.pdf.**

Welcome, Wolf!

Welcome to a fun and exciting year of Cub Scouting, Wolf! You will go on adventures, exploring the world around you with other Wolves in your den. You will play games, make fun things, learn about wildlife, and spend lots of time outdoors. Best of all, you'll even earn awards while having all this fun!

Cub Scouting

Do you know how many years Cub Scouting has been around? Cub Scouting began in 1930, which means it is now more than 80 years old. Can you imagine how many boys have been Cub Scouts in all those years? If you said "tens of millions," you would be right!

Lord Baden-Powell founded the Scouting movement in 1907. Over time, programs started for younger boys.

Baden-Powell really liked the stories in *The Jungle Book* by Rudyard Kipling, and he thought many of the characters were fun and playful, just like Cub Scouts. He also knew it was important for the boys to have a wise leader like Akela (Ah-KAY-la), the wolf. Akela lets Mowgli (MO-glee), the boy, join the wolf pack. Maybe you also know about Baloo the bear, who helps teach Mowgli the laws of the jungle so he can live among the animals. To this day, we have names like Akela and Baloo, and words like den and pack, in Cub Scouting. That's our way of remembering how Cub Scouting began with *The Jungle Book*.

Your Wolf Leaders

In a real wolf pack, all the wolves look to their leader for guidance—when to work, when to learn, and when to play. A leader like Akela makes sure each young wolf learns about the world and how to get along with other members of the pack.

As a Wolf Scout, you have several people who you can call "Akela." These include the den leader, the assistant den leader, and your parent or guardian. Akela can be anyone who is older than you and a wise teacher, just like Akela in *The Jungle Book*.

These leaders help you to learn new things, and they can even help you find new ways to use what you have already learned! Akela will also sign your adventure requirements in the handbook when you complete them.

Did you know you can also help lead your den by becoming a denner? The denner is a Scout usually chosen by the members of his den to help the den leader and den chief at meetings and outings and serves for about one to two months. If you're elected to be the denner, do your best!

Your Wolf Den and Den Meetings

Being a Wolf in the Boy Scouts of America means that you belong to a den of boys who are Wolves just like you! These boys are in the same grade or are the same age as you, and you all come together in "den meetings" a few times a month. In these meetings you will work on the Wolf adventures, earning awards, playing games, and making fun things with the rest of the den.

Your Pack Meetings

You, your family, and your den also go to a monthly pack meeting. This is a meeting for all the boys in all the dens in the pack to get together at the same time. It's a chance to tell others about the hard work your den has done on the adventure that month, and also a time for awards and seeing what other Scouts in the pack are doing, at all different rank levels.

Your Wolf Uniform

Your uniform is an important part of being a Cub Scout. Wearing it lets people know that you belong to a Wolf den and a pack and, most important, you belong to the Boy Scouts of America! You should wear the uniform to den meetings, pack meetings, and any special activities you participate in as a Wolf.

The official uniform for Cub Scouts includes blue Cub Scout pants or shorts and shirt with insignia for your rank. Each rank has its own neckerchief and slide in the rank colors and a belt buckle to be worn with the blue Cub Scout belt. Wolf Scouts can also wear an official navy-blue cap with a yellow front panel and Wolf emblem. When you wear the full Cub Scout uniform, it shows you are a member of the team.

The pictures below show you where to put the Wolf Scout insignia on the sleeves and pockets of your uniform.

You might receive an emblem for participating in day camp or a council popcorn sale. This is an example of "temporary insignia" and should be worn centered on the right pocket.

The denner wears gold shoulder cords suspended from the left shoulder of his uniform. The cords are removed when his time as the denner ends.

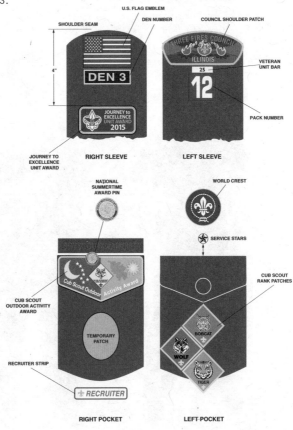

Character Compass

As you work on your Wolf adventures in your *Wolf Handbook*, you will notice this symbol:

A compass is a tool that guides a person from place to place. Character is how we act, and it guides our entire lives. This compass will be your guide to one or more of the 12 points of the Scout Law. Every time you check the compass, it will remind you of how the activities in each adventure are related to the Scout Law. This may also help you think about how the points of the Scout Law guide our way in Cub Scouting and in daily life. Those points are all different, and each one is a treasure for you to find.

THE OUTDOOR CODE

Much of Scouting, including Cub Scouting, happens outside. For more than 60 years, the Outdoor Code has been a guide for Scouts in the outdoors. Remember to do your best by showing respect for the outdoors and by learning and upholding the Outdoor Code.

THE OUTDOOR CODE

As an American, I will do my best to—

+ Be clean in my outdoor manners,
+ Be careful with fire,
+ Be considerate in the outdoors, and
+ Be conservation-minded.

Being clean in your outdoor manners, careful with fire, and considerate means you can enjoy the outdoors in ways that do no harm to the environment. Being conservation-minded encourages the protection and thoughtful use of natural resources and doing your part to improve the condition of the land and the environment.

As a Cub Scout, you will learn to use the Leave No Trace Principles for Kids to help you take care of an area where you hike or camp.

LEAVE NO TRACE PRINCIPLES FOR KIDS*

Leave No Trace™
Center for Outdoor Ethics | LNT.org

1. **Know Before You Go.** Find out about the place you're going to camp ahead of time. Are there rules you need to know about? Are any activities against the rules? Is water available? Do you need to bring anything special?

2. **Choose the Right Path.** Always walk on trails, even if that means getting your boots muddy. Don't take shortcuts. Set up tents in marked camping areas.

3. **Trash Your Trash.** Use bathroom facilities when available. Follow campground rules for handling dishwater. Pack out all your trash unless the campground has trash pickup.

4. **Leave What You Find.** Leave any natural treasures where you find them so other campers can enjoy them, too. If you want a souvenir of your campout, take a picture. A good saying to remember is "Leave nothing but footprints, take nothing but pictures, kill nothing but time."

5. **Be Careful With Fire.** Cook on a camp stove or grill whenever possible. It's easier and less messy than cooking over an open fire. Only build fires in designated fire rings. Always have someone keep an eye on your fire until it is dead out.

6. **Respect Wildlife.** Travel quietly and give animals enough space that you don't disturb them. Getting too close to an animal can potentially hurt the animal and you. Take pictures from a safe distance. You're visiting the animal's home, so be considerate.

7. **Be Kind to Other Visitors.** Be respectful of other visitors by keeping noise down and not entering other groups' campsites without permission. Be polite to other people you meet. Give them the respect you expect from them.

To help you remember the Outdoor Code and the Leave No Trace Principles for Kids, you can find them in the back of your handbook.

The member-driven Leave No Trace Center for Outdoor Ethics teaches people how to enjoy the outdoors responsibly. This copyrighted information has been reprinted with permission from the Leave No Trace Center for Outdoor Ethics: www.LNT.org.

Your First Rank—Bobcat!

If you haven't earned your Bobcat badge yet, this is where you start. When you've earned your Bobcat, you'll know the signs, symbols, and big ideas of Scouting. And when you know those, you're a Scout!

If you haven't already earned your Bobcat badge, you will start your Cub Scouting adventures by learning what it takes to become a Bobcat.

Read through the Bobcat requirements and practice several times what you have learned. When you think that you are ready, share what you've learned with your family, your den leader, and with your den at a pack meeting. Then give yourself a pat on the back and congratulate yourself on earning your Bobcat badge.

BOBCAT REQUIREMENTS

1. Learn and say the Scout Oath, with help if needed.
2. Learn and say the Scout Law, with help if needed.
3. Show the Cub Scout sign. Tell what it means.
4. Show the Cub Scout handshake. Tell what it means.
5. Say the Cub Scout motto. Tell what it means.
6. Show the Cub Scout salute. Tell what it means.
7. With your parent or guardian, complete the exercises in the pamphlet *How to Protect Your Children From Child Abuse: A Parent's Guide.*

One of the most important parts of earning Bobcat is understanding that all members of the Boy Scouts of America believe in, live by, and often repeat the Scout Oath and the Scout Law. We learn those words and believe in them as a way to live our lives and be good members of our families, our communities, and the Boy Scouts of America.

Scout Oath

On my honor I will do my best
To do my duty to God and my country
and to obey the Scout Law;
To help other people at all times;
To keep myself physically strong,
mentally awake, and morally straight.

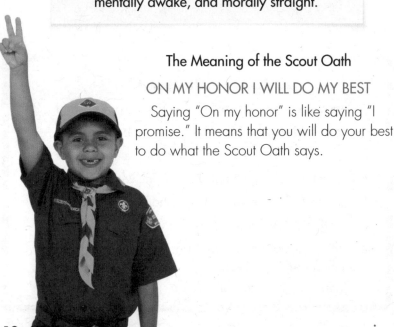

The Meaning of the Scout Oath

ON MY HONOR I WILL DO MY BEST

Saying "On my honor" is like saying "I promise." It means that you will do your best to do what the Scout Oath says.

The Scout Oath has three promises.
Let's look at what they mean.

TO DO MY DUTY TO GOD AND MY COUNTRY AND TO OBEY THE SCOUT LAW

A duty is something you are expected to do. At home, you might be expected to make up your bed or take out the trash. You also have duties to God and to your country. You do your duty to God by following the teachings of your family and religious leaders. You do your duty to your country by being a good citizen and obeying the law. You also promise to live by the 12 points of the Scout Law, which are described on the next page.

TO HELP OTHER PEOPLE AT ALL TIMES

Many people need help. A friendly smile and a helping hand make life easier for others. By helping other people, you are doing a Good Turn and making our world a better place.

TO KEEP MYSELF PHYSICALLY STRONG, MENTALLY AWAKE, AND MORALLY STRAIGHT

The last part of the Scout Oath is about taking care of yourself. You stay physically strong when you eat the right foods and get plenty of exercise. You stay mentally awake when you work hard in school, learn all you can, and ask questions. You stay morally straight when you do the right thing and live your life with honesty.

Akela's OK　　　　**Date**　　　**Den Leader's OK**

Scout Law

A Scout is trustworthy, loyal, helpful, friendly, courteous, kind, obedient, cheerful, thrifty, brave, clean, and reverent.

The Meaning of the Scout Law

The Scout Law has 12 points. Each is a goal for every Scout. He does his best to live up to the Law every day. It is not always easy to do, but a Scout always tries.

A Scout is TRUSTWORTHY. A Scout tells the truth and keeps his promises. People can depend on him.

A Scout is LOYAL. A Scout is true to his family, friends, Scout leaders, school, and country.

A Scout is HELPFUL. A Scout volunteers to help others without expecting a reward.

A Scout is FRIENDLY. A Scout is a friend to everyone, even people who are very different from him.

A Scout is COURTEOUS. A Scout is polite to everyone and always uses good manners.

A Scout is KIND. A Scout treats others as he wants to be treated. He never harms or kills any living thing without good reason.

A Scout is OBEDIENT. A Scout follows the rules of his family, school, and pack. He obeys the laws of his community and country.

A Scout is CHEERFUL. A Scout looks for the bright side of life. He cheerfully does tasks that come his way. He tries to make others happy.

A Scout is THRIFTY. A Scout works to pay his way. He uses time, property, and natural resources wisely.

A Scout is BRAVE. A Scout can face danger even if he is afraid. He stands for what is right even if others laugh at him.

A Scout is CLEAN. A Scout keeps his body and mind fit. He helps keep his home and community clean.

A Scout is REVERENT. A Scout is reverent toward God. He is faithful in his religious duties. He respects the beliefs of others.

Akela's OK   Date   Den Leader's OK

3 | Show the Cub Scout sign. Tell what it means.

   Make the sign with your right hand. Hold your arm straight up.
The two raised fingers stand for the Scout Oath and the Scout Law.
The fingers look like the sharp ears of the wolf ready to listen to
Akela! Remember that Akela means "good leader" to a Cub Scout.
Your mother or father or guardian is Akela. So is your Cubmaster
or your den leader. At school, your teacher is Akela.

| Akela's OK | Date | Den Leader's OK |

When you shake hands with another Cub Scout, do this: Hold out your right hand just as you always do to shake hands. But then put your first two fingers along the inside of the other boy's wrist. This means that you help each other to remember and obey the Scout Oath and Scout Law.

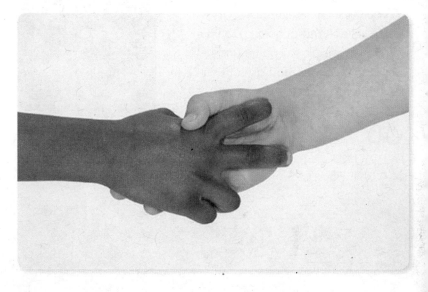

Akela's OK   Date   Den Leader's OK

The Cub Scout motto is "Do Your Best."

A motto is a guiding principle and a rule for living. Do Your Best means trying your hardest, not just a little bit. Do your best all the time. Do your best in school and at home. Do your best when you play a game and help your team. Do your best as you work on your rank adventures!

_____   _____
Akela's OK   **Date**   **Den Leader's OK**

Salute with your right hand. Hold your first two fingers close together. Touch your fingertips to your cap. If you aren't wearing a cap, touch your right eyebrow. You salute the flag to show respect to our country. Always use the Cub Scout salute when you are in your Cub Scout uniform, both indoors and outdoors. If you are not in uniform, you salute the flag by placing your right hand over your heart.

Akela's OK	Date	Den Leader's OK

7 | **With your parent or guardian, complete the exercises in the pamphlet *How to Protect Your Children from Child Abuse: A Parent's Guide.***

If your handbook does not include the pamphlet, talk with your den leader.

7 _____   _____
Akela's OK   Date   Den Leader's OK

Congratulations on earning your Bobcat badge! You may now continue on the trail of your Wolf adventures. Let's take a look at what those adventures are called, what you need to do to earn your Wolf badge, and all the fun things you will explore as a Wolf.

BOBCAT ®

The Wolf Adventures and Requirements

The requirements to earn your Wolf rank may be completed in any order. Akela (your den leader, parent, or guardian) will decide on the order for your den. You can do the electives any time you want. And you'll earn an adventure loop for each adventure you complete.
Let's go, Wolf!

WOLF RANK REQUIREMENTS

1. Complete each of the following Wolf required adventures with your den or family:

 Call of the Wild

 Howling at the Moon

 Council Fire

 Paws on the Path

 Duty to God Footsteps

 Running With the Pack

2. Complete one Wolf elective adventure of your den or family's choosing. (See page 29.)

3. With your parent or guardian, complete the exercises in the pamphlet *How to Protect Your Children from Child Abuse: A Parent's Guide* and earn the Cyber Chip award for your age.*

* If your family does not have Internet access at home AND you do not have ready Internet access at school or another public place or via a mobile device, the Cyber Chip portion of this requirement may be waived by your parent or guardian.

WOLF ELECTIVE ADVENTURES

 Adventures in Coins

 Germs Alive!

 Air of the Wolf

 Grow Something

 Code of the Wolf

 Hometown Heroes

 Collections and Hobbies

 Motor Away

 Cubs Who Care

 Paws of Skill

 Digging in the Past

 Spirit of the Water

 Finding Your Way

Once you have achieved all of the Wolf rank badge requirements and your handbook has been signed, you are ready to earn your Wolf badge! Let out a big GRAND HOWL, Wolf Scout!

CALL OF THE WILD

I couldn't wait to go on my pack's first camping trip last year. In fact, I was so excited that I forgot one pretty important thing: my sleeping bag!

Luckily, some Scouts in my pack had extra blankets. Our Cubmaster showed us how to make a sleeping bag out of the blankets. Do you know what? It was pretty comfortable! We had a blast on the campout, and I never forgot my sleeping bag again. Now I make a list and check everything off before I leave. Are you ready to head out into the wild, Wolf?

SNAPSHOT OF ADVENTURE

You are about to leave on another great adventure—camping with your family or pack. Before you go, plan what you need to bring. Your parent or guardian and den leader will help you get ready. But each time you go camping, you can show you are a Wolf Scout by doing more on your own. You will also learn more about the animals you may see, how to tie a few basic knots, how to prepare for the weather, and how to handle possibly harmful situations. Let's go, Wolf!

Telling stories, toasting marshmallows, looking at the stars, sleeping in a tent... These are just a few of the activities waiting for you when you camp out with your pack friends and your family.

But before you go, what should you bring? Start with the Cub Scout Six Essentials:

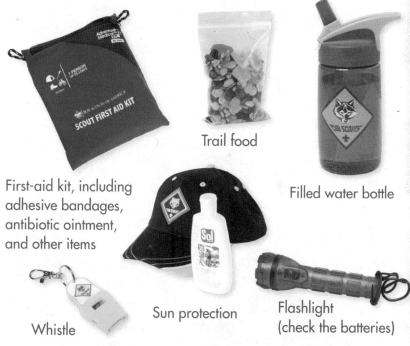

Trail food

First-aid kit, including adhesive bandages, antibiotic ointment, and other items

Filled water bottle

Whistle

Sun protection

Flashlight (check the batteries)

Now, make a complete list of what you need to bring when you camp with your pack or with your family. The list on the next page includes items you might want on a family or pack campout. Discuss with your pack or your family which items are needed.

Make a check mark next to the items you plan to bring.

- [ ] Sleeping bag (or blankets to make blanket beds)
- [ ] Underwear
- [ ] Socks
- [ ] Pajamas
- [ ] Knife, fork, spoon
- [ ] Plates, bowls, cups
- [ ] Trash bag
- [ ] Insect repellent
- [ ] Toothbrush and toothpaste
- [ ] Toilet paper
- [ ] Sweater or jacket
- [ ] Poncho or raincoat

- [ ] Bar soap
- [ ] Towel
- [ ] Extra pants and shirts, if rain is likely
- [ ] Extra pair of shoes
- [ ] *Wolf Handbook*
- [ ] Bible, testament, prayer book, or other book for your faith

GROUP EQUIPMENT CAN INCLUDE:

- [ ] Cooking pot or pan
- [ ] Pliers for dipping dishes in hot rinse water
- [ ] Plastic sheet for air-drying dishes
- [ ] Charcoal (camp stove if not using wood fire)
- [ ] Food for all camp meals
- [ ] A cooler to keep perishable foods cold
- [ ] Waterproof groundsheets
- [ ] Tents
- [ ] Hammer for stakes

When you go camping for the first time, you can often use borrowed or substitute equipment. A plastic groundsheet is nice, but an old shower curtain works well, too. For many Scouts, their first mess kit is a plastic bowl that used to hold whipped dessert topping. As you go camping more often, you can add to your equipment.

Before you leave on your campout, check off the list to make sure you have everything. Make sure your gear works and you have all the poles and stakes you need to set up your tent. If you can, check the weather right before you leave to make sure you know the latest conditions. If anything can change quickly, it's the weather! Have a great time, Wolf!

Akela's OK   Date   Den Leader's OK

REQUIREMENT 2 | Show how to tie an overhand knot and a square knot.

Tying knots is an important Scout skill. It is also something you will use throughout your life. Some of the knots you will learn in Scouting have been used for thousands of years.

Every knot has a special purpose. Some knots join pieces of rope together. Some knots that don't slip are used for rescues. Other knots are perfect for tying down equipment—you can adjust these knots and they will still hold.

OVERHAND KNOT

An overhand knot is simple. You can use it to keep a rope from going through a pulley, a hole, or to make a rope easier to grip.

An overhand knot is also the first step for some other knots. You will need a single strand of rope to practice this knot.

1. First, make a loop in the end of a rope.

2. Next, tuck the end of the rope through the loop.

3. Pull the end of the rope to tighten the knot.

Hint: Do you need a larger knot to stop a rope from going through a big hole? You can make a larger stopper knot by adding a second overhand knot after the first one.

SQUARE KNOT

The main use of a square knot is to join the ends of two ropes. This is why it is called the joining knot in Scouting.

You can use both ends of one piece of rope to make a square knot or two different colored pieces of rope.

1. Hold one end of a rope in one hand and the other end of the rope in your other hand. (Or hold a different colored rope in each hand.)

2. Bring the right side rope over the left side rope. Go under and around the left side rope with the right side rope.

3. Now bring the left side rope over the right side rope. Go under and around the right side rope with the left side rope.

4. Pull both ends firmly. The knot will not hold its shape without being tightened.

You can use a square knot to tie bundles together. You also use the first half of a square knot when you tie your shoelaces.

Remember, the square knot is not to be trusted when safety is important. Just like your shoelaces, a square knot can sometimes come undone.

An easy saying to help you remember the steps for a square knot is: "Right over left and under, and left over right and under."

 You can find more cool knots to master (with a parent's permission) at **boyslife.org/video-audio/644/learn-to-tie-knots/** or in books at **www.scoutstuff.org.**

A Scout who knows his knots and when to use them will be a great help on Scouting adventures!

Akela's OK   **Date**   **Den Leader's OK**

I always have to practice tying a new knot a lot before I get it right. The first few times I tried a square knot, I made a jumbled mess out of it. Then I couldn't untie the weird knot I had made! I finally wiggled the knot free so I could try it again. I was "knot" happy ...haha!

When you are outdoors, you share the area with animals that live there. They may be birds, mammals, insects, reptiles, or other creatures. Knowing the animals that live in an area is a way for Wolf Scouts to be prepared. For example, when you are camping in some parks and wilderness areas, you may have to use a bear bag or take other steps to keep your food safe from animals.

Learning more about the animals that live near you is also an important outdoor skill. The more you know, the more connected you will feel to the place where you live and the natural world around you.

Instead of saying, "I saw a butterfly," you can say, "I saw a monarch butterfly with orange and black wings." In learning to identify a monarch butterfly, you might also learn that monarchs, like many birds, fly south in the fall and north in the spring. In fact, monarchs can migrate more than 2,500 miles a year!

Your den leader or another adult will help you learn about the
animals that live nearby. Make a list below. Write down how you
can identify each animal.

	Animal	How I can identify it
1.	_____	_____
		_____
2.	_____	_____
		_____
3.	_____	_____
		_____
4.	_____	_____
		_____

Camping is great when you are ready for any kind of weather. If you get caught in a rain shower in a T-shirt, you will be sopping wet and cold. But if you have rubber boots and a waterproof jacket and pants, you can keep on having fun!

With your den leader or parent, talk about the different kinds of weather that could happen where you are going to camp. Can the temperature or weather change a lot from morning to night? Make a list below of possible weather you could run into. Write the gear you will bring along to be prepared for the weather.

Weather	What I will bring to be prepared
_____	_____
_____	_____
_____	_____

Akela's OK   Date   Den Leader's OK

A. When a stranger approaches you, your family, or your belongings.

B. In case of a natural disaster such as an earthquake or flood.

C. To keep from spreading your germs.

Being prepared also means knowing how to keep yourself safe and healthy. Here are some ways to prevent danger, injury, and sickness in the outdoors.

NO, GO, YELL, TELL!

When you are at any Scout event, **stay with a buddy—always!** Buddies that stick together are much safer.

Remember to check first with the person in charge before going anywhere with anyone. If anyone approaches you and asks you to go somewhere with them, you should take a few steps back from the person so you have room to move and room to think. Say, "I need to check first," and go directly to an adult in charge to check in.

If someone is trying to force you to go somewhere with them without checking first, remember, "No, Go, Yell, Tell!"

◆ Say **"NO!"** loudly.

◆ **GO** away. Run if you have to.

◆ **YELL** loudly for help. Screaming sounds like playing, so yell from your gut.

◆ **TELL** your parent, den leader, or another adult you trust right away.

Even if you freeze in the moment or forget to get away, know that it still isn't your fault. You can still TELL even a long time after something happened. With your parent or den leader, practice the steps of "No, Go, Yell, Tell!"

 A Scout is obedient. Following directions is part of keeping yourself (and your friends and fellow Scouts) safe.

NATURAL DISASTERS

Ask your den leader or someone in your family what types of natural disasters have happened where you live. Talk about what you can do to be prepared. If a disaster ever happens, what can you do to protect yourself?

In any natural disaster, staying calm will help you stay safe.

Each type of natural disaster may also call for certain actions. For example, if you are camping near a river or creek and it floods, you may only have moments to run to higher ground.

Put a check mark beside the disasters that could happen near you. In the space to the right, write down one thing you can do to stay safe if this kind of disaster happens.

Natural Disaster	One thing I can do to stay safe
☐ Flood	_____
☐ Earthquake	_____
☐ Wildfire	_____
☐ Blizzard	_____
☐ Hurricane	_____
☐ Tornado	_____

THE BEST WAY TO STAY WELL?
WASH YOUR HANDS!

It isn't fun to be sick on a campout! The best way to stay healthy and to keep from spreading germs is to wash your hands often with soap and water. This is true no matter where you are. Follow these steps to show you know the proper way to wash your hands. Always wash your hands after you use the restroom and before you eat or you help cook a meal.

Use soap.

Rub for 20 seconds.

Rinse.

Dry with a towel.

Turn off the faucet with a towel.

A Scout is courteous. When you wash your hands, you are being polite to others around you.

_____   _____
Akela's OK   **Date**   **Den Leader's OK**

Campfire shows are a perfect way to spend an evening laughing, singing, and having a good time under the open sky. You and your family or your den may want to plan ahead to learn a fun song or make up a skit to perform at the campfire show.

What does your family like to do outside? Fishing? Camping? A sport? Is there a funny song you can think of or a skit you can make up about a favorite family outdoor activity?

You can find lots of fun campfire songs in the *Cub Scout Songbook* before you go. Or brainstorm with your group to come up with an entertaining idea for a skit or song at the campout!

Akela's OK   **Date**   **Den Leader's OK**

As a Scout, it is your job to help leave any park or camping area better than the way you found it. Learn the Outdoor Code so you'll be ready. You can find the Boy Scouts of America's Outdoor Code in the back of your handbook.

One part of the Outdoor Code is a promise to be careful with fire. When you are safe with fire, you are being clean in your outdoor manners, considerate in the outdoors, and conservation-minded.

CAMPFIRE SAFETY

Always have adult supervision for campfires. Only build fires in an approved place on gravel, sand, or bare soil that is far away from trees or brush.

adult supervision

water nearby

small fire

ground cleared of materials that will burn

Put out every fire when you no longer need it. Make sure it is completely out. The ground where the fire was burning should be cold. Clean up the campfire site and return any materials you moved to their original places. The site should look just as it did when you arrived.

CAMP STOVE SAFETY

Sometimes a camp stove will be used for cooking. There are also rules to keep you safe around a camp stove.

1. Only use camp stoves with help from an adult.
2. An adult should always fill and light the stove.
3. Watch out for long or baggy sleeves when you are cooking.

7A

Akela's OK   **Date**   **Den Leader's OK**

REQUIREMENT 7B | Recite the Leave No Trace Principles for Kids with your leader. Talk about how these principles support the Outdoor Code.

The principles of Leave No Trace help Scouts and others enjoy time in nature without causing harm to it. There are seven Leave No Trace Principles for Kids, and they share many of the same goals as the Outdoor Code.

Find the principles in the back of your handbook, and recite them with your den leader. Can you see how these principles will help you live out the Outdoor Code? With your den leader, discuss ways that you will demonstrate the principle "Be Careful With Fire" on your campout.

7B

_____   _____
Akela's OK   Date   Den Leader's OK

REQUIREMENT 7C | After your campout, list the ways you demonstrated being careful with fire.

Think about the times you were near the campfire or a stove on your campout. Explain to your den leader how you followed the Outdoor Code and the Leave No Trace Principles for Kids by being careful with fire. In the space below, write what you did.

I was careful with fire when I...

_____

_____

7C   Akela's OK   **Date**   **Den Leader's OK**

_____   _____

"When I woke up after my last campout and saw all of the packs, coolers, camp stoves, and tents, I thought it would take us forever to clean up. But it was amazing how quickly we all worked together to pack. And when we finished, you never would have known we were there. I felt proud that we were taking care of the campsite and living the Outdoor Code. It even felt like the animals in the trees were watching us and giving us a "paws-up" for taking care of their home. Camp on, Wolf!

COUNCIL FIRE

Boy Scout service project,
Memphis, Tennessee, 1940s.

When I did the Council Fire adventure, I learned a lot about the ways my town has changed. I found old pictures of the town when there were just a few buildings. My school was just a big field!

I'm proud that my Wolf den's community service project helped improve a wildlife habitat. We planted native plants to create a better home for the animals that live there. We also picked up a bunch of junk and brought it to a recycling center. Scouts can make a big difference in helping our communities!

SNAPSHOT OF ADVENTURE

A real wolf pack works like a large family where everyone works together to keep the members of the pack safe, healthy, and happy. Working together is part of being a good citizen. When your own pack has a job to do, Akela calls the pack together and leads a council fire. At a council fire, members of the pack share ideas. They figure out how to get the job done together. In this adventure, you will be a part of different packs—your den, your pack, your family, and your community.

I pledge allegiance to the Flag of the United States of America, and to the Republic for which it stands, one Nation under God, indivisible, with liberty and justice for all.

Learning how to show respect for the flag and how to care for it are parts of being a good citizen.

One way American citizens show respect is by having a flag ceremony. Your leader will show you the steps of the ceremony and the proper way to fold the flag.

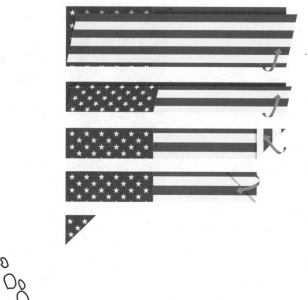

Akela's OK	Date	Den Leader's OK

REQUIREMENT 2 | Work with your den to develop a den duty chart, and perform these tasks for one month.

Like any team, your Wolf den has to work together to get things done. Chores get completed faster and are more fun when you're working with your Wolf buddies.

With your den leader, make a list of the things that have to be done every week before and after your den meeting. Do you move tables and chairs together that must be put back after your meeting? Do you need to clean up after your meeting? Did you work on a craft or have food and drinks? Do you have den supplies to take care of?

Work with your den to figure out a duty list. Your den leader will give each den member a job to do from this list. Each Wolf will have a job to do for the next month. Pitch in and be cheerful! Remember to finish your duty each time you meet.

Akela's OK   Date   Den Leader's OK

NOTE TO AKELA: Help your Wolf find an old picture and one recent photo of your community. Check the local library, local newspaper, or the Internet.

How would you describe the community where you live? Is it a big city, a small town, a suburb, or in a rural area?

Have you ever looked around your community and noticed that something is different? Maybe an empty lot is now a playground. Or maybe a new school was built in a place that was once a field. Towns and cities are changing all the time. And there is a good chance that your community looks very different from the way it looked many years ago.

Salt Lake City between 1870 and 1890

Salt Lake City, 1904

Salt Lake City, present day

Wichita, Kansas, 1880

Look for pictures and stories about your community when it was first settled or early in its history. Perhaps you can find old postcards that show how your town looked long ago. You might be able to take a picture of the same location now to show how it has changed! Or look for photos of your town that have been taken recently. With your parent's help, you can find a lot of interesting facts and pictures about your community at your local library.

Create a project to show how your town has changed, and share it with your den. Discuss with your den how your community has changed over time.

3A _____ _____
Akela's OK   Date   Den Leader's OK

REQUIREMENT 3B | Select one issue in your community, and present to your den your ideas for a solution to the problem.

Every community has to deal with issues—important subjects or problems that people talk about to decide what to do. Sometimes, people have very different views on what should be done. With your parent's help, use local news from TV, newspapers, or the Internet to learn about issues in your community.

For example, if you live in an area that is growing a lot but has experienced a long drought, one issue may be the water supply. What does your town plan to do so that everyone in the future has enough water? Does your community encourage people to conserve water? What is good and bad about the plan?

Maybe your town has a lot of old buildings that are empty and in need of repair. Do some people want to repair them, but others want to tear them down and build bigger, modern buildings?

Now think about the issue yourself. What do you think should happen? Why? When you meet with your den, share your ideas for solving this issue with your den leader. Listen quietly to everyone's ideas. Are there different ways to solve the problem? Can you see why people must work together toward a common goal to solve community issues?

TOWN NEWS ★★★ Final edition

Community Center Plans
A town meeting will be held next week to discuss

3B   Akela's OK   Date   Den Leader's OK

A wolf pack in the wild has a leader. Your Scout pack is led by a pack committee that makes decisions. Look at the ideas for community service projects below. After your den has chosen one, write down a few notes about the project to share with the pack committee.

Here are some ideas for community service projects:

1. Plant a tree (or two or three) that is native to your area.

2. Clean up a vacant lot, or paint over graffiti on a wall.

3. Plant flowers that are native to your area in a public place.

4. Volunteer your den's time to help out at a food bank or host a food drive.

5. Help clear a trail of trash and debris, or clean up along the banks of a local creek.

6. Visit a senior center.

7. Help your chartered organization by performing yardwork.

Present your den's ideas clearly to the pack committee. Tell them if your den needs help with a certain task.

The pack committee will talk with you about your ideas and help you figure out the best plan.

Akela's OK　　　　**Date**　　　**Den Leader's OK**

58 ▪ Wolf

REQUIREMENT 4B | Work together on a community service project.

Now that your den has met with the pack committee, it is time for everyone to pitch in on a community service project. You and your Wolf den will feel great when you work together to make your community a better place!

A Scout is loyal. When you work with your den on a community service project, you are showing that you are loyal to your community.

You and your den should bring along any supplies needed to complete your service project. Be sure to get permission in advance from those in charge of the location before you start.

A good service project takes planning with your den to make it a big success! Be proud of what your Wolf den can do to help your community.

4B

_____   _____
Akela's OK   Date   Den Leader's OK

In the wild, adult wolves in a pack work together to protect the whole pack from danger. Men and women keep our communities and our country safe by serving as law enforcement officers, emergency care providers, firefighters, and military service members.

When you meet with a first responder, community worker, or military veteran from your area, shake hands and thank the person for his or her service. Ask about the reasons he or she became a public servant or volunteered to serve in the military. Find out more about the work he or she does to improve the community or keep us safe here at home.

After you meet with a public servant or military veteran, write and send a thank-you note. Say thank-you for taking the time to meet with you. Be sure to express your appreciation to the person for his or her service.

Akela's OK   **Date**   **Den Leader's OK**

My den met with the director of our town's parks department. He takes care of all of the parks in our town and plans events at them. He said the parks help people stay healthy and give wildlife a place to live. The festivals are fun, too! My family spends a lot of time at the town parks, so his job is important to me. In fact, I'm on my way to try a new skate park now!

Americans buy a lot of stuff. We also throw away a lot. When you practice the three R's, you are helping to create less garbage and take care of our environment.

Following the three R's also means we create less pollution. The factories that make products like paper, plastics, and aluminum use chemicals, water, and energy.

Cars, trucks, trains, planes, and ships that use gasoline and oil also create pollution. Moving products from factories to stores uses energy and causes pollution. When a product is used and thrown away, it can stay in the environment for a long time.

Did you know that every plastic bottle that has been thrown away in the last 50 years is still around today? Remember, you may drink a soda in 30 minutes, but the plastic bottle it came in will be around for the rest of your life.

PRACTICING THE THREE R'S

Reduce means using less. For example, if you use a cloth towel instead of a paper towel, you use fewer paper products that have to be thrown away.

You can also reduce how much water you use. Turn it off while you are brushing your teeth. Take short 5- to 10-minute showers, just long enough to get your body clean and your hair washed.

Turn off the lights when you leave a room. This reduces the amount of energy it takes to run your house. It will also help your family reduce the electric bill!

Reuse means to use something again. If you use a sandwich container that can be washed and reused, you will use fewer plastic bags that cannot be recycled.

Take reusable bags with you when your family goes shopping. Plastic bags end up in landfills.

Refillable bottles

Reuse empty cans and jars for storing crayons, markers, and other small stuff. Before you throw something out, think about how you could use it in a new way!

Recycle means collecting things that can be made into something else. That keeps these items from going to a garbage dump. Plastic bottles, cans, cardboard, newspaper, glass jars, and many other items we use every day can be recycled.

Collect recyclables in bins at your house or take them to a local recycling center. Use recycling bins at school and in your community, too.

How does recycling work? Here's one example:

1. Plastic bottles are sent to a recycling center and are sorted by type and color.

2. The plastic is cleaned and chopped up into tiny pieces.

3. The tiny pieces are melted into a liquid.

4. The liquid is spun into fibers, like thread.

5. The fibers are woven into fabric that can be made into clothing.

If your family needs to recycle old computers, phones, TVs, paint cans, or chemicals, ask your parent to see if there is a special recycling center nearby for those items.

Choose one way to reduce, one way to reuse, and one way to recycle. Every little bit helps save our land, air, and water, and helps wildlife have a clean place to live, too. Make the three R's a habit!

Akela's OK	Date	Den Leader's OK

I found out that my favorite fleece jacket was once a bunch of plastic bottles. It's so awesome that the bottles are now keeping me warm instead of sitting in a landfill!

REQUIREMENT 6B | Make your own recycling center, or contribute to an existing one.

Community recycling centers often recycle paper, plastic, aluminum, and other things. Ask your parent or den leader what you can take to your local center.

Your den may decide to make its own recycling center. Many Scout dens and troops work with organizations to recycle items that would otherwise wind up in landfills. A den or troop can collect items such as candy wrappers or empty juice boxes. Then the den can ship them off to be recycled or transformed into new products.

With your den, make containers to collect recyclables in your home, your classroom, your den, your parent's workplace, or somewhere else in your community. Your recycling center may collect telephone books, newspapers, eyeglasses, old cellphones, or other recyclables. Work as a group to gather and take these things to your local recycling center.

A Scout is thrifty. When you reduce, reuse, and recycle items, you are being thrifty by using resources carefully and not being wasteful.

Akela's OK	Date	Den Leader's OK

Toys. Art. Boats. Furniture. Stained-glass windows. Treehouses. Hundreds of cool projects have been made from recycled materials. Bring to your den meeting items that would have been thrown away—and bring your imagination!

With your den, brainstorm what you can make from the items everyone brings. Use the best ideas to create a project from recycled objects. Display your project at a pack meeting.

Akela's OK	Date	Den Leader's OK

DUTY TO GOD FOOTSTEPS

Have you ever thought about the footsteps you take every day? Sometimes when I'm trekking to school or the park, I'll start to think about people who took the same steps a long time ago. Things were pretty tough for them! I wonder how they kept going and stayed strong when they had so many hard things to deal with.

My brother once said that they had faith in their beliefs. Then they took the first step to live out that faith—and just kept going. That's pretty great, if you ask me. Now I'm learning ways to live out my own beliefs through stuff I do with Cub Scouts and my family. What footsteps will you take today, Wolf?

SNAPSHOT OF ADVENTURE

Faith means having belief in God and doing your duty to God. Practicing your faith also means sharing with others what you believe through your actions. In this adventure, you will find out how some people have shown their faith in the past. You will  learn ways to share your own faith. In Scouting, boys are challenged to take footsteps to find their own duty to God. The steps of faith you take each day will help you become a more caring and reverent Scout.

DUTY TO GOD—RELIGIOUS EMBLEMS

Many faith-based organizations have religious emblems and programs designed for different grade levels. Contact your faith leader or, with your parent's permission, visit **www.praypub.org** or **www.scouting.org/filestore/pdf/512-879_WB.pdf** for further information.

Many people throughout America's history have placed their faith in God. In good times and in bad, in times of war and peace, they believed that God would see them through the challenges they faced.

There are many religious monuments and historic sites that honor people for their service. Some mark great battles and terrible sacrifices made by Americans. Others are the sacred places of people who have always called America home: the American Indians. Some sites are places of worship where people gather to pray and reflect on their faith.

Gettysburg Cemetery

At such sites, we can learn more about people of faith and remember them with respect and reverence. These sites also help us think about the footprints these people left in their journeys through life.

A Scout is reverent. Visiting places that honor people of faith is one way to show reverence.

Robert Baden-Powell started Boy Scouts in England more than 100 years ago. He taught Scouts to be reverent toward God, to respect each other's religion, and to treat each other like brothers.

"Every Scout should have a religion," he said. "Religion seems a very simple thing: First: Love and serve God. Second: Love and serve your neighbor."

There is a museum about Baden-Powell's life at the National Scouting Museum in Irving, Texas. Scouts who visit the museum can pay their respects to Baden-Powell as the founder of Scouting.

Now it is your turn to visit a religious monument or historic site near where you live. Take photos or draw some pictures. What impressed you about the place you visited or the person or people honored there?

Akela's OK	Date	Den Leader's OK

A great way to remember a trip is to take photos or draw pictures. With your den or your family, put together a visual display that tells the story of your trip.

Show how the visit made you feel reverent or strengthened your faith in God.

Akela's OK	Date	Den Leader's OK

My family and I visited an outdoor chapel made more than 100 years ago. Then we built a model of it at home using rocks and cardboard. I took it to a den meeting to show my den. What did you make for a visual display of your trip?

REQUIREMENT 2 | Complete 2A and at least two of requirements 2B-2D.

REQUIREMENT 2A | Give two ideas on how you can practice your duty to God. Choose one, and do it for a week.

When you practice your faith, you strengthen your belief in God and show your duty to God. Can you be counted on to tell the truth? Do you show God's love to those around you? Do you respect your parents or guardians? Are you a good friend to everyone? Do you practice kindness, self-control, patience, and goodness? Do you set a good example for others? Do you treat others as you wish to be treated?

There are many ways to practice duty to God.

If you have a friend who is worried about something, you can share how praying to God helps you when you are worried or scared. You can include that person in your prayers at home, too.

If your family attends a place of worship regularly, you might invite a friend and his or her family to attend with you. Introduce them politely to your family and others. Make them feel welcome!

Do you have a neighbor or a friend who needs your help? Think about what you can do to help out your family, your friends, and your neighbors without being asked.

 A Scout is kind. Showing kindness to others is one way many people demonstrate their duty to God.

Giving thanks before meals or saying a prayer before bed each evening or when you get up in the morning is another way you can practice your faith.

What are your ideas for practicing your duty to God? Which one did you choose to do for a week?

Idea 1: _____

_____

Idea 2: _____

_____

Other Ideas: _____

_____

2A   **Akela's OK**   **Date**   **Den Leader's OK**

Many people overcame great difficulties to come to America so they could practice their religions freely. Many of the first 13 colonies were formed so people of different faiths could practice their religious beliefs. These people were persecuted, or treated badly, in their home countries in Europe because of their faiths.

From the earliest days in our country's history, American citizens demanded that their personal freedoms should be protected, including their right to practice their religion. The First Amendment to the U.S. Constitution does just that! It protects freedom of speech, press, religion, assembly, and petition.

William Penn

America has become a melting pot of people from different backgrounds and many faiths. You may want to read about the Pilgrims who came to America from Europe almost 400 years ago. Or look for stories about modern-day people seeking religious freedom who came here from countries around the world.

With help from your parent or guardian find and read a story about people who came here seeking religious freedom. Talk with your family about what you learned.

| Akela's OK | Date | Den Leader's OK |

Choose a song that shows reverence or duty to God. It might be a song you can sing as a grace before meals, or one that encourages someone. It might be a morning song to help you prepare for the day ahead. Or it might be an evening song to help you thank God for all that happened that day. You can find many songs of faith in the *Cub Scout Songbook*.

Sometimes, songs of hope and faith are written during difficult times to show patriotism, respect for our nation, and reverence for the bravery of our people.

Some patriots believed that God played an important part in battles in our nation's history. Did you know that the "Battle Hymn of the Republic" was written to encourage soldiers to believe in God's presence with them during the Civil War?

With your family or den, sing the song you selected.

Akela's OK	Date	Den Leader's OK

REQUIREMENT 2D | Offer a prayer, meditation, or reflection with your family, den, or pack.

In Scouting, we use prayers to show reverence. We also use them to give thanks for the things we learn, for our parents, for our Scouting leaders, and for our Scouting friends. We show our respect to God when we pause and offer thanks for our blessings and opportunities.

You can make up your own simple prayer to say with your family, den, or pack. You can also find interfaith prayers in the BSA pamphlet "A Scout Is Reverent." Have your parents or guardians help you select some that support your family's beliefs.

Here are some interfaith prayers from a BSA website:

+ For health, strength, and daily food, we give you thanks, O God.

+ For this and all your mercies, God, make us truly grateful.

+ For food, health, and friendship, we give you thanks, O God.

@ You can find also find interfaith prayers in the BSA pamphlet "A Scout Is Reverent" or, with a parent's or guardian's permission, at **www.scouting.org/filestore/pdf/Interfaithservice.pdf.**

Different faiths have different customs when they pray. Some faiths have special head coverings, and some raise or cross their arms when they pray. Others kneel on special rugs. Follow the guidelines of your family's faith when you pray, and be respectful of how other Scouts show their faith.

Akela's OK   **Date**   **Den Leader's OK**

My older brother is a leader in his Boy Scout troop. He went to the Summit Bechtel Family National Scout Reserve for a high-adventure camp. He taught me a prayer he learned there, and I said it to my Wolf den last year. It really made me think about how thankful I am that we both love Scouting and being outdoors. Here is the prayer he taught me:
For this time and this place,
For Your goodness and grace,
For each friend that we embrace,
We thank Thee, O God.
Amen

HOWLING AT THE MOON

Being in skits is so much fun! This year, I played the part of a nervous mouse in a skit with my den. I made up a squeaky voice, put on mouse ears, painted whiskers on my face, and pinned a tail on the back of my pants. Every time another character moved, I jumped sideways and squeaked like crazy. Everyone laughed. My den leader said I was so good as a mouse, he might ask me to play the part of a prairie dog in our next campfire skit!

SNAPSHOT OF ADVENTURE

For many years, people believed that wolves howl at the moon. Wolves actually howl to communicate with one another. For example, a wolf might howl to mean, "I want to meet up with the pack," or "Here's where I am." During this adventure, you will get a chance to do your own howling. You will show you can communicate in different ways, create and perform a skit, and help put on a Wolf campfire show.

How can you make someone who does not speak your language understand you? Can you act out a story without speaking? Can you draw a picture?

There are four different ways to communicate:

1. **Verbal communication** is when you use your voice to communicate, like when you talk and sing.

2. **Non-verbal communication** uses facial expression, body language, and motions to communicate without words.

3. **Written communication** is just that. People write in letters, emails, books, magazines, newspapers, and material on the Internet.

4. **Visual communication** includes graphs, charts, maps, photographs, and art to tell stories.

How many of these ways do you use to communicate?

People who are deaf or hard of hearing cannot hear what others say. Many speak using another type of language called American Sign Language (ASL). You can learn the Cub Scout motto in American Sign Language.

Cub Scout   Motto

Do   Your   Best

Plains American Indian Sign Language is a type of sign language created long ago by American Indians. It uses hand gestures to communicate whole words. It is easy to learn and a fun way to communicate with your den while hiking or watching wildlife. You can even learn the sign for "Wolf"!

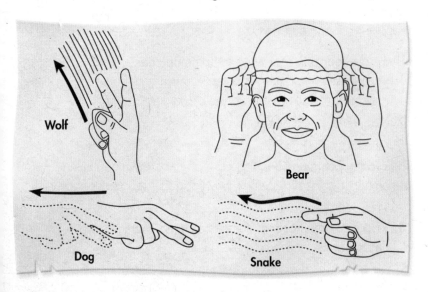

Wolf

Bear

Dog

Snake

With your den, you will complete an activity where you cannot see or speak. You will wear a blindfold, and a buddy will lead you through an obstacle course. Share what you had to do to communicate.

A Scout is helpful. If someone is having difficulty communicating, be helpful by listening carefully and patiently. Remember, not being understood can be frustrating.

_____   _____
Akela's OK   **Date**   **Den Leader's OK**

REQUIREMENT 2 | Work with your den to create an original skit.

Get ready to communicate "fun"! Create an original skit with your den. Skit ideas can come from your imagination, jokes from books or *Boys' Life* magazine, and Scout skits. If you use a Scout skit, you can change the characters to fit the size of your den. Your den leader may suggest topics or ideas.

Skits are very short, somewhere between 90 seconds and 5 minutes long. Brainstorm with your group to decide the best way to present the skit. Keep it simple! Listen to everyone's ideas as you decide on a plan. Each Wolf should take part in some way. Who will play each role?

While you plan and practice your skit, keep the Scout Law in mind. Use only language and actions that reflect the beliefs of Scouting and leave everyone—actors and audience—with smiles on their faces.

Practice as a group, and be sure to learn your lines. Remember to speak up so your audience can hear you. How will you make your character come to life with your voice and your gestures?

Stay in character. That means that if you are playing the part of a duck, you should walk, talk, and act like a duck the entire time you are performing. Have fun with your performance, and your audience will enjoy it, too!

Akela's OK   Date   Den Leader's OK

REQUIREMENT 3 | Work together with your den to plan, prepare, and rehearse a campfire program to present to your families at a den meeting.

Now it is time for you to howl! One of the places Scouts howl is at a campfire—a Scouting tradition. A campfire program brings Scouts, parents, and leaders together to have fun!

There is a legend about how Scouts started having campfire fun. The legend has been passed down to Wolf Scouts each year. This tradition started a long time ago. Now it is your time to learn about it!

THE STORY OF THE LONE WOLF

Once upon a time, many, many years ago, a wolf cub lived in a forest near some tall mountains. This wolf cub belonged to a pack. Then one night there was a terrible storm. All of the wolves ran to seek shelter, but this wolf cub was not a fast runner. He became separated from the pack and was left behind in the woods. All of the trees began to look alike, and he did not know which way his friends had run.

The wolf cub lived by himself and felt very alone. One cool, dark night he looked around and was surprised to see something shining at the top of a mountain. He decided to climb the mountain to find out where the light was coming from. As he climbed, he felt the light getting brighter. When he reached the top, he saw

a campfire. He found light and warmth, and these made him happy. He let out a long howl to say, "Look at me here, with this warm fire. Everyone is welcome to join me."

As if by magic, a small pack of wolves appeared from the dark forest. They gathered around the fire. The lone cub was so happy to see them that he let out a howl and they all joined in, as if in song. Their song was a happy one. They howled and danced around the fire. This was the first campfire song! After their howling song, one of the wolves went to the center of their circle. He raised his paws and applauded with joy. He told his friends their song was fun. This was the first campfire cheer!

The lone cub wanted to know where these wolves had come from. The pack was excited to tell their story. But their way of telling the lone cub their story was new to him. Each of the members of the pack acted out a part. The lone cub liked watching each of the wolves help tell their story. This new way to tell a story became known as a skit.

In fact, he was so happy to watch their story that, after their tale, he jumped up and did a flip! This was the first stunt ever to be performed at a campfire!

When they asked the lone cub why he was alone, he told his story. He said he was sad to be alone. He told his new friends that his story had a happy ending since he had so much fun at their campfire.

The wolves fell asleep until the sun tickled their noses to signal the morning. They gathered together and invited the lone wolf cub to join their pack. They all prepared to find their way down the mountain.

The lone cub stayed for a little longer, thinking about the fun night he had spent with his friends. He felt as if the campfire had been magical, and he did not want to lose that magic.

He paused. Before leaving, he scooped up some of the cool ashes from the campfire and placed them carefully in his neckerchief. He tied a square knot in the neckerchief and put it around his neck. He thought, "I will carry the spirit of the campfire with me always. The next time I have a campfire,

"I will put these ashes in it so that campfire will be full of this cheerful spirit." And then he ran away to join his new pack!

And that is the legend of how the campfire tradition began!

Did you notice what happened during the wolf campfire? The lone wolf called others to come to the campfire. Then the wolves sang, cheered, acted, and even did some stunts! The campfire ended with a story. Think about what you will need to do to prepare for a campfire with your den.

OPENING

The lone wolf howled or signaled to the other wolves. Just as wolves use their sounds to signal to other wolves, you use your voice to give messages to Scouts in your den or pack. When you gather around a campfire, you will need a way to get everyone's attention so the campfire program can begin. We call this an opening. Openings can be very simple with just saluting the flag, praying, or reciting the Scout Oath and Scout Law. What are some ways you could open your campfire program?

SONGS

The wolf pack all howled together in a circle. Now that you have everyone's attention, it is time to sing a fun song! Action songs get everyone up and moving. They energize the group so

everyone is ready to have lots of fun. Think about a song that you have sung in your den or pack meetings. Pick one that you like to sing, or learn a new song.

CHEERS, STUNTS, AND RUN-ONS

One wolf danced around with a howl to applaud the rest. Cheers, stunts, or run-ons are other fun parts of a campfire. (Run-ons are short, silly skits.) All these things keep everyone paying attention. And they make people laugh! With the help of your den leader, learn how to lead a cheer, stunt, or run-on, and then teach it to others in your den or pack.

A Scout is cheerful. When you laugh and join in at a campfire, you are showing your Scout spirit.

SKITS

The wolf pack acted out how they arrived at the top of the mountain. One of the best traditions of a campfire is performing skits. You have probably already done skits with your den. For the campfire program you are planning, create a new skit with your den.

STORY

The lone wolf told his story. Near the end of the campfire, someone tells a story. Listening to a story gives everyone a chance to settle down, relax, and enjoy the fading flames of the campfire. The story might be a legend, a tall tale, or a true story. What kinds of stories do you like to hear?

CLOSING

The flames of the fire went out as the wolf cubs went to sleep. After the story, it is time to close the campfire. At this point, the flames are fading. With your den leader, choose a way to end your campfire program.

Collecting ashes from campfires has been a Scouting tradition for many years. The morning after your campfire, when the ashes are cool, collect some ashes from the campfire with your den leader or another adult. Save them to sprinkle on your next campfire to keep the Scouting spirit alive, just as the lone wolf cub did in the legend.

3   Akela's OK   Date   Den Leader's OK

Our Wolf den put on a cowboy campfire program. We sang a cowboy song called "Tumbling Tumbleweeds." We put on a funny skit about cowpokes who were so sore from riding horses on a cattle drive that they could hardly move. We did rope tricks and told cowboy jokes! What did you do for your campfire program?

What role will you play in your pack campfire program? How will you learn your lines or the words to a campfire song? Sometimes the best way to learn something is just to say it or do it over and over again until you have it down. A few minutes of practice can make a big difference in the way you feel when you perform.

When you work with your den on a campfire program, be trustworthy by doing what you say you will do. Each Wolf needs to do his part to make the program great.

You might also want to practice your lines with someone in your family or in front of a few people you know before you do it for your pack.

It is not always easy to go in front of a group and perform. In fact, sometimes it might make you feel a little nervous.

Everybody gets stage fright. It usually passes quickly, almost as soon as you start to perform. Take a few long, deep breaths before you begin. Sometimes just taking a sip of water before you start will help you do your best. Remember that your audience is there to listen to what you are going to say. They want to have fun, and they want you to have fun, too!

There will be many times in Scouting where you will be asked to speak or perform in front of others. The skills you learn will help you in school, in your community, and in many different areas of your life.

The role I performed in my pack campfire program was

_____.

4   **Akela's OK**   **Date**   **Den Leader's OK**

Campfire shows and skits are so cool! Did you have fun howling at the moon, Wolf?

PAWS ON THE PATH

Every hike is a new adventure—you never know what will happen! Some surprises are fun, like spotting an eagle. Other surprises remind you why the things we learn in Scouting are so important.

When my Wolf den went hiking last year, it was early spring. First, we met with the park ranger. He told us that the trail we had planned to take was closed to repair a bridge. He showed us another short trail on a park map that we could hike instead. Our den leader said that it's always a good idea to check in with a park ranger before you hike in a state park, to let someone know where you plan to go, and to check trail conditions. I'm sure glad we did!

SNAPSHOT OF ADVENTURE

Exploring far-away mountains. Traveling through deep, dark jungles. Crossing hot, dry deserts. The adventurers that mastered these journeys got their start on a short hike, just like the one you and your Wolf den are about to take! In this adventure, you will use your Scouting outdoor skills and learn more about the natural world around you. Hike on, Wolf!

The success of a trip often depends on what you carry with you, whether it is in a backpack or on a pack animal.

It is important for you to have items with you to take care of any minor emergencies that could happen, even on a short, 1-mile hike! Cub Scouts who have hiked before you came up with a great list of items to bring. They are called the Cub Scout Six Essentials.

Round up these items, and place them in a backpack before you start out on a hike with your Wolf den.

FIRST-AID KIT

A kit should include a few adhesive bandages, some moleskin (a sticky bandage that you can put over a blister to keep it from getting worse or rubbing), and soap or hand sanitizing gel.

FLASHLIGHT

Check your batteries to make sure they have plenty of juice. Your flashlight will be used only in an emergency, so save the batteries for times when you really need them!

FILLED WATER BOTTLE

You should bring enough water for you to drink through your whole hike and back. And make sure your bottle is full when you start out! It is not safe to drink water you find along the trail. Your den leader can help you decide how much water you should bring.

TRAIL FOOD

Trail mix or a granola bar provides quick energy when you need it.

SUN PROTECTION

Sunscreen should be SPF 30 or greater. A hat is good to have, too!

WHISTLE

It's only for emergencies, but a whistle will last longer than your voice.

You might want to pack an extra pair of socks in case your feet get wet or it rains. A rain poncho, waterproof jacket, or even a large plastic garbage bag with holes cut out for your head and arms will keep you dry if it rains. What other gear should you take on your hike? Remember, you'll have to carry it all yourself and bring it all back!

1

Akela's OK   **Date**   **Den Leader's OK**

"Two heads are better than one." You may have heard that saying before, and it is true. Sometimes you may forget a safety rule, or not be aware of a hazard up ahead, but if you are with a buddy, it is easier to stay safe.

The buddy system is a great way for Scouts to look after each other, especially on outdoor adventures. When you go hiking, swimming, or camping with your den, each Scout is assigned a buddy. You keep track of what your buddy is doing, and he knows at all times where you are and how you are doing.

A Scout leader might call for a buddy check. That means you must immediately hold up the hand of your buddy. If a Scout is missing, everyone will know it right away. The buddy system is a way of sharing the good times and keeping everyone safe.

My buddy on the hike was _____

_____   _____
Akela's OK   **Date** · **Den Leader's OK**

A Scout is brave. When you go hiking, always stay with your buddy and your den. If you do get lost, be brave and stay put until you are found. Learn how to "S-T-O-P" on the next page.

REQUIREMENT 3 | Describe what you should do if you get separated from your group while hiking.

A Wolf should always stay with the rest of the group while hiking. If you do find yourself and your buddy (because you always have one, right?) away from the rest of your den, here is what you need to do:

S - T - O - P!

S = Stay calm. Stay where you are. Sit down, take a drink of water, and eat a little trail food. Stay where you can be seen. Don't hide! You are not in trouble!

T = Think. Think about how you can help your leaders or others find you. Stay where you are, and be sure people can see you. Make yourself an easy target to find. Remember, people will come to look for you. Stay put, be seen, and help them find you!

O = Observe. Listen for the rest of your group or people looking for you. Blow your whistle three times in a row, then listen. Three of any kind of signal means you need help, and everyone will try to help you.

P = Plan. Stay calm, stay put! Plan how to stay warm and dry until help arrives. Don't worry, you will be found.

S – T – O – P! works if you ever get separated from your family, too.

Akela's OK   Date   Den Leader's OK

REQUIREMENT 4 | Choose the appropriate clothing to wear on your hike based on the expected weather.

Talk with your den leader about what kind of clothing to wear on the hike. What you need to wear will depend on the season and where you live. It is also important to think about what time of day you will be hiking. Layering is a good way to dress for places where the weather can be cold, hot, and in between, all in one day.

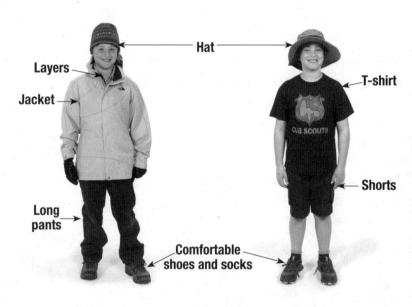

Layers — Hat — T-shirt
Jacket
Long pants
Comfortable shoes and socks
Shorts

4   Akela's OK   Date   Den Leader's OK

Cub Scouts love to be outdoors. But getting to enjoy all of the fun and excitement of nature also means taking care of it.

The Outdoor Code is a way for every Scout to be a part of keeping our world beautiful and safe—today and for years to come.

Read the Outdoor Code below, and practice saying it out loud. Then, recite the Outdoor Code with your den leader.

OUTDOOR CODE

As an American, I will do my best to—
Be clean in my outdoor manners,
Be careful with fire,
Be considerate in the outdoors, and
Be conservation-minded.

The Leave No Trace Principles for Kids also help us take care of the outdoors. You can find them in the back of your book. One of those principles is "Respect Wildlife."

Read the actions below:

- If an action shows respect for wildlife, mark a ✔ in the box.
- If an action does not show respect for wildlife, mark an **X** in the box.

Share with your den leader, parent, or guardian the choices you made in preparation for your hike in requirement 6.

Action	Respects Wildlife
Chasing a deer off of the path	
Keeping empty snack wrappers to throw away at home	
Watching a bug with a magnifying glass	
Shouting loudly to a friend down the trail	
Leaving wildflowers where you find them	
Feeding some of your snack to a squirrel	

After completing your hike in requirement 6, reflect on the Outdoor Code and Leave No Trace. With your den leader, discuss ways that you and your den were considerate in the outdoors by respecting wildlife.

5

Akela's OK   **Date**   **Den Leader's OK**

REQUIREMENT 6 | Go on a 1-mile hike with your den or family. Watch and record two interesting things that you've never seen before.

It's time to put your paws on the path and take a hike with your den or your family, Wolf!

Studying a map will help you understand the land and see where you will be hiking. With your family or your den, look at a map of the area where you will be hiking. You might be able to answer these questions.

♦ Does the trail have a name?

♦ Is the trail made of dirt, concrete, or another material?

♦ Is it flat or will you be climbing hills?

♦ Is there a river, creek, or other body of water around?

♦ Will you hike in one direction and then turn around and come back, or does the trail make a circle?

♦ Which direction is north?

Sometimes forks in the trail aren't marked with signs showing you which way to go. That's when a map can really come in handy! When you are in doubt, stop and check the map to help you stay on the right path.

Your leader or parent will tell you the rules for hiking. Be sure to follow them so everyone has a great time. You might want to do some leg and arm stretches and a few knee bends before you start out, just to get your body warmed up.

Walk at a steady pace, stay with your buddy, and leave a couple of feet between yourself and the next Wolf on the trail. Give everyone space to enjoy the woods quietly. Stop and rest when needed. Make sure you have your water bottle(s) and drink when you are thirsty.

Look and listen for birds, mammals, insects, and other creatures along the way. Use your eyes, ears, and sense of smell to enjoy nature all around you. See if you can spy two interesting things that you have not seen before.

Two interesting things I saw on the trail:

1. _____

2. _____

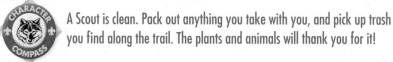

A Scout is clean. Pack out anything you take with you, and pick up trash you find along the trail. The plants and animals will thank you for it!

Akela's OK   Date   Den Leader's OK

Whether you live in a city, in a suburb, on a farm, by the ocean, or in the mountains—birds, bugs, and other animals live there, too. What kinds of creatures live near you?

With your parent's or guardian's permission, go to the library or on the Internet and find information about your local wildlife. Write down two types of birds, two insects, and two other animals that live near you.

BIRDS

Do the birds that you picked live near you all the time or do they migrate (travel) there for part of the year? What do they eat? What kinds of trees or bushes do they like to nest in? Do both the male and female help build the nest and raise their young?

INSECTS

Are there bees, wasps, ants, flies, roaches, beetles, or butterflies near you? Bugs are fascinating creatures! Did you know that bees can fly up to 60 miles a day to gather food? Or that ants can lift more than 50 times their own weight? What did you find out about the two insects that you chose?

OTHER ANIMALS

Some wild animals have figured out how to live around people. Coyotes, foxes, possums, raccoons, squirrels, rabbits, deer, and other species of animals may be close by. What kinds of animals live near you?

Tell how the animals you studied can be identified. Share what you found out with your den leader.

Write down the two birds, two insects, and two other animals you learned about that live in your area.

Birds _____

_____

Insects _____

_____

Other animals _____

_____

Akela's OK   **Date**   **Den Leader's OK**

REQUIREMENT 8 | Draw a map of an area near where you live using common map symbols. Show which direction is north on your map.

A map is a small illustration of a large area of land. Maps can help you figure out where something is located. They can also help you give directions to other people.

Many people look at a map before they start out on a trip so they can visualize (see) where they are going. Some hikers like to look at a computer screen or use a Global Positioning System (GPS) device to help them plan their outing.

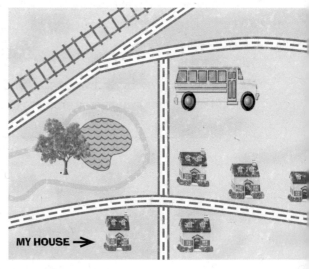

With your parent's or guardian's help, look up a map of your town or an area near where you live. Maps use different symbols to show where roads, rivers, lakes, and other large features are located.

The map symbols are shown in a "key," which is a box that tells what they mean. Reading a map is easy when you can use the key. Work with your parent or guardian to learn what the symbols on a map mean.

Look for a compass rose on the map. A compass rose is a circle or a design with points to show directions on a map. Maps are usually oriented toward true north, which will be found at the top of the compass rose.

When north is at the top of the compass rose, south will be at the bottom. East is on the right and west is on the left.

When you draw your map, show which direction is north. You will learn how to use a compass with your den so you can orient a map to north.

8   Akela's OK   **Date**   **Den Leader's OK**

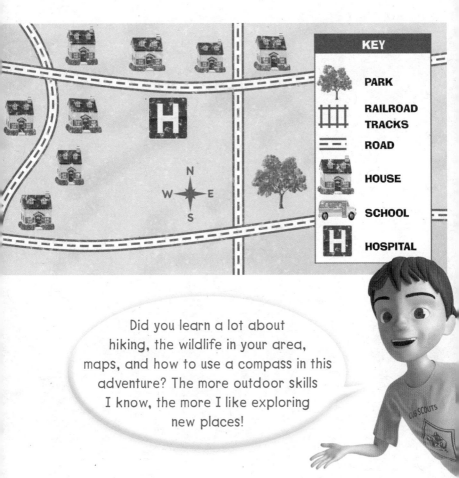

KEY

PARK

RAILROAD TRACKS

ROAD

HOUSE

SCHOOL

HOSPITAL

Did you learn a lot about hiking, the wildlife in your area, maps, and how to use a compass in this adventure? The more outdoor skills I know, the more I like exploring new places!

RUNNING WITH THE PACK

I started being more active when I became a Wolf. The first time I tried to run, I had to stop before I got to the end of the block. I really wanted to be able to keep up in games, so I practiced running and did other active stuff. Most of the time, I felt like I was just playing and having fun. But I was actually getting stronger!

Now I can go a lot farther. I feel better, too. Do you feel good after you exercise? Let's learn some fun ways to get moving, Wolf!

SNAPSHOT OF ADVENTURE

Wolf Scouts lead happy, active lives! Catching, throwing, balancing, and stretching will help you run with your Wolf pack wherever you go. The more you move, the more you will improve! In this adventure, you will practice your Wolf athletic skills and show you know how to eat nutritious food to keep your body running in tip-top shape.

REQUIREMENT 1 | **Play catch with someone in your den or family who is standing 10 steps away from you. Play until you can throw and catch successfully at this distance. Take a step back, and see if you can improve your throwing and catching ability.**

When you can follow a ball with your eyes, catch it easily with your hand, and throw it accurately, you are learning a great skill. It is called eye-hand coordination. Before you know it, you will be throwing and catching like a true ball player.

If you have never played catch before, use a soft, squishy ball at first so that nobody gets hurt. If you don't have a baseball glove, you can play catch with your bare hands. Just make sure you use a soft ball, not a baseball, to practice.

HOW TO THROW A BALL

◆ Gently hold the ball in your throwing hand. Step forward on the opposite foot.

◆ Bring the ball behind your ear with your elbow pointing backward.

- Turn your body to the side so that the shoulder opposite the ball faces the target. If you are throwing with your right hand, the person catching should be to your left. Never throw a ball with your chest facing the target.

- Point to the other person with your free hand. Then throw. It may take a little practice to throw the ball where you want it to go.

HOW TO CATCH A BALL

- If you are playing with bare hands, reach out with both hands to catch the ball. If you are using a baseball glove, catch the ball in the pocket of the glove. Put your other hand over the ball to keep it from rattling around in the glove or falling out.

- If the ball is thrown to you above your waist, place both of your bare hands in front of your body, fingers up, to catch the ball. Keep your eyes open. If you are using a baseball glove, place the glove in front of your body, glove hand up, to catch

the ball. When the ball is inside your glove, put your other hand over the ball to keep it there.

♦ If the ball comes toward you below your waist, bend at the knees and keep the upper part of your body straight. Watch the ball. Catch the ball with both bare hands in the underhand position or with your glove hand in the underhand position. If you are using a glove, cover the ball with your opposite hand.

PRACTICE PLAYING CATCH!

Once you are comfortable throwing and catching a soft ball, play catch with a family member or someone in your den. If you are playing with bare hands, use a soft, squishy ball for safety. Play catch with a baseball only when you have a baseball glove to catch it.

Start by standing three steps away from someone in your den or family. Throw the ball toward the other person. When the other person catches it, he or she throws it back to you. Each time the ball comes back to you and you catch it, take one step back.

Keep throwing, catching, and stepping back until you are 10 steps away from the other person. Play until you can catch and throw easily from this distance without dropping the ball on the ground. Then, keep taking steps back after you make a catch. See how far you can go!

Akela's OK   Date   Den Leader's OK

REQUIREMENT 2 | Practice balancing as you walk forward, backward, and sideways.

Hiking on a rocky trail. Riding a bike down the street. Walking up and down stairs. These activities all take balance. Balance training is important to everyone, from kids playing games to serious athletes.

Balance helps us stand up straight. It also helps us walk, run, and sit. By practicing balance exercises, you won't fall over as much. And that keeps Cub Scouts in the game!

Here are some exercises to improve your ability to balance:

Walk at least six steps in a straight line on the ground. Go forward and backward. Do it sideways, too. Then try the same steps while walking on a board. Put your arms out to the side to help you stay balanced. Stare at a single focal point, and limit your head and eye movements. This is how tightrope walkers and gymnasts keep their balance.

When our den did the balancing exercises, we also tried to stand up tall, close our eyes, put our hands out to the sides, and hold one leg up for five seconds. It was a lot tougher than it sounds! Try it and see how you do.

Akela's OK	Date	Den Leader's OK

It is fun to do front rolls, back rolls, and frog stands! They also show you are limber and have good balance. Be sure to tuck your chin to your chest when you do front and back rolls. This protects your neck and makes it easier to roll. Do your best!

Frog stand

Front roll

Back roll

3   **Akela's OK**   **Date**   **Den Leader's OK**

REQUIREMENT 4 | Play a sport or game with your den or family, and show good sportsmanship.

Playing sports and games is a great way to be active and it's also a chance for tons of fun. Choose a sport or game to play with your family or den. Then get your paws moving, Wolf!

While you're playing, remember that Scouts practice good sportsmanship whenever we play together! Good sportsmanship teaches you teamwork, understanding, patience, respect for others, and many more important qualities.

Good sportsmanship means treating those we play with as we would like them to treat us. Use encouraging words, help out your teammates, and be a good winner or loser. This is all part of being a good sport.

Check the ways that you showed good sportsmanship with your family or den.

☐ I stayed calm.

☐ I treated others kindly.

☐ I listened to the adult leaders.

☐ I followed the rules.

☐ I stayed positive.

☐ I encouraged my teammates.

☐ I was friendly after winning or losing.

Remember, a good sport has fun because he enjoys playing the game more than he cares about the score!

A Scout is friendly. Being a good sport means being friendly and kind to others when you play a sport or a game.

4   Akela's OK   Date   Den Leader's OK

Walking like different animals lets you use your muscles in different ways. These are fun exercises to try with your den members. They will also help you move quickly, improve your balance, and get stronger. Hop to it, Wolf!

Frog leap

Inchworm walk

Kangaroo hop

Crab walk

5   **Akela's OK**   **Date**   **Den Leader's OK**

Exercise helps keep us strong. So does choosing nutritious food from the five food groups. You don't have to have food from each group at every meal. But you should try to choose foods from each group every day. Talk with your parent or guardian about how you can eat a balanced diet. With his or her help, plan a healthy meal for your family.

There are five food groups: fruits, vegetables, grains, dairy, and protein. You know what fruits and vegetables are. Grains are foods like rice, wheat, oats, cornmeal, and barley, just to name a few. Bread, pasta, and oatmeal are all foods made from grains. The dairy group includes milk, yogurt, and cheese. Meat, chicken, fish, eggs, nuts, and beans are all in the protein group.

The United States Department of Agriculture has made it easier for kids to learn how to choose healthy foods by creating a My Plate chart that shows you what you should eat and how much of your plate should be filled with the five food groups at meals.

Here are some tips to help you plan a good, nutritious meal for your family:

♦ **Eat more fruits and veggies.** Make half of your plate fruits and vegetables every day!

♦ **Try whole grains.** Ask for oatmeal, whole-wheat breads, or brown rice at meals.

♦ **Rethink your drink.** Drink fat-free or low-fat milk or water instead of sugary drinks.

♦ **Focus on lean protein.** Choose protein foods like beans, fish, lean meats, and nuts.

♦ **Slow down on sweets.** Eat sweets, like cakes or cookies, once in a while and in small amounts.

Akela's OK	Date	Den Leader's OK

When I was a Wolf Scout last year, our den leader challenged us to replace our bad habits with good habits. Now, instead of sitting on the couch, my friends and I play outside whenever we can. My mom also stopped buying sugary drinks—and I don't even miss them! How will you get moving, Wolf?

ADVENTURES IN COINS

SNAPSHOT OF ADVENTURE

To most people, coins are used to buy things you want or need. But coins can also tell a story. The pictures on U.S. coins tell a lot about our country's culture and history. They feature important Americans and also include pictures of animals, art, buildings, and science.

In this adventure, you will get to be a numismatist (noo-MIZ-muh-tist). Phew! Can you say "numismatist" five times fast? A numismatist is a person who studies coins and money. You'll learn where coins are made and the meaning of their pictures and words. It's time to make some cents, er, sense out of coins!

Look at the stone in the picture. It is a kind of money called a rai stone that weighs thousands of pounds. Can you imagine putting that kind of money in your pocket?

REQUIREMENT 1 | Identify different parts of a coin.

Many things have been used for money. Some were useful, like salt, animal hides, and arrowheads, which were traded for other items people needed. Other objects used for money, like shells, had no real value but became symbols of wealth in some countries.

Salary is the payment we receive for doing work. The word comes from the Latin word sal, or "salt." In ancient Rome, it meant the amount of money given to a Roman soldier to buy salt.

Even before it was made into coins, metal was used for money. Long ago, each tiny piece of metal had to be weighed every time it was used to figure out its value. Soon, the custom of stamping the weight on the metal became widely used. It made the pieces of metal easier to use for buying and selling things.

It is a mystery who invented the first coins. Experts believe the first coins were minted, or made from metal, in the region around ancient Greece. It wasn't long before many countries were making coins by hand that showed pictures of their rulers and animals.

Modern American coins are made by machines. However, artists design the coins, and scientists work hard to improve how they are made.

Look at a coin. What is special about it? See how many parts you can name.

The **bust** is a picture of a person's head.

The **legend** is the main writing.

The **field** is the background of the coin.

The **relief** is all of the raised parts of the coin.

The **inscription** is writing on the coin.

The **mint mark** is a letter telling where the coin was made.

The **edge** is the outer surface of the coin. It could have lettering, designs or ridges on it.

The **rim** is a raised area near the edge around the coin on both sides. It helps the coin keep from wearing out too quickly.

Ridges on the outer edge of the coin can be felt by rubbing your finger across it. They look like lines imprinted on the side of the coin. The ridges, or milling, were included on coins to keep dishonest people from shaving off the edge of a coin to use the precious metal for other purposes.

Now that you have learned the parts of a coin, share what you learned with your den leader or a parent or guardian.

Akela's OK   Date   Den Leader's OK

Did you know that the U.S. Mint makes 65 million to 80 million coins each day? That's a lot of pocket change!

The job of the U.S. Mint is to make the coins that Americans use. Coins in the U.S. are only made in its secure facilities. (Paper money is made in the Bureau of Engraving and Printing.)

Most coins have a mint mark, a letter below the date that tells where they were made. Four facilities make coins and use mint marks.

They are:

Philadelphia = P	San Francisco = S
Denver = D	West Point = W

Denver

Today, only the mints in Philadelphia and Denver make circulating coins. Circulating coins are the coins at a bank, in a cash register, or in people's pockets that are used to buy things.

San Francisco

Philadelphia

U.S. Mint
in Denver

The San Francisco and West Point mints only make coins for collectors. These coins could be used as money, but many collectors keep them in their original packaging and never touch them. They hope that the rare coins will become more valuable over time.

In the past, other U.S. Mint locations made coins. It is possible you might see one of their mint marks on a coin, such as New Orleans, Louisiana, "O"; Charlotte, North Carolina, "C"; and Carson City, Nevada, "CC". You may even find some coins with no mint mark at all!

Now look for the date on the coin. The date of issue is the year the coin was produced. It is usually found on the front of a coin, but on quarters in the 50 State Quarters® Program, the date is on the back of the coin. Isn't it amazing how much you can learn from looking closely at a single coin?

Akela's OK   Date   Den Leader's OK

REQUIREMENT 3 | Play a coin game.

You may have played a game of "heads or tails" before. A person flips a coin up in the air and you call "heads" or "tails." If you call "heads" and the coin lands with the side with the head (or bust) facing up, you win the coin toss.

Coin games have been around just about as long as coins have! Did you know that a coin toss has decided which team will kick off the football game since the start of professional football in 1892?

Now it's time to try a few coin games with your family or den!

Here are two examples you can try:

Coin Basketball Sit down at a table with a large coin (a quarter or half dollar). Place a cup about 2 or 3 feet in front of you. Hold the coin upright on its rim between one finger and thumb. Try tossing the coin into the cup. You can also try bouncing the quarter off a table and into the cup. Just as in basketball, give yourself two points every time you make it in the cup.

Coin Kick Each player is given a coin to place on the toe of his shoe. He then raises his foot and "kicks" the coin into a pie tin.

Akela's OK   **Date**   **Den Leader's OK**

COOL COIN FACTS

Each U.S. coin represents a part of a dollar and shows the faces of famous Americans.

Cent The one-cent coin is often called a penny. The inside of a cent is made with zinc. Then the zinc is coated with copper. The cent features the 16th president, Abraham Lincoln. Some of the designs are shown here.

1909–1958: Two ears of wheat symbolize America's abundance.

1959–2008: One-cent coins have the Lincoln Memorial on the back.

2009: The back shows scenes from Lincoln's life.

 Lincoln's birthplace in Kentucky

 Lincoln as a youth in Indiana

 Lincoln as a lawyer in Illinois

 Lincoln's presidency in the White House

 2010–present: The shield shows the union of states.

Five-cent piece The nickel is worth 5 cents. It is made of copper and nickel, which is how it got its name. It features President Thomas Jefferson and his home, Monticello.

Dime The dime is worth 10 cents and is also made of copper and nickel. It features President Franklin Roosevelt on the front. The back features several items: a torch, which stands for liberty, is in the center; an olive branch for peace is on the left side; and an oak branch for strength is on the right.

Quarter The quarter is worth 25 cents or one-fourth of a dollar and is also made of copper and nickel. It features the first U.S. president, George Washington, on the front of the coin. The back of the coin has one of more than 100 different designs, such as a majestic eagle, an outline of a state, U.S. territories, national parks, or the Bicentennial of 1976.

The Bicentennial Quarter celebrates 200 years of American freedom.

State quarters show unique facts about each state.

America the Beautiful Quarters® show national parks and sites in each state; Washington, D.C.; and the U.S. territories.

 U.S. Territories Quarters honor the District of Columbia, Puerto Rico, Guam, American Samoa, U.S. Virgin Islands, and Northern Mariana Islands.

What is on the back of your state's quarter? What does it show about the history or culture of your state?

Half-dollar The half-dollar, or 50-cent piece, is made of zinc and nickel. It features President John F. Kennedy on the front and the eagle from the presidential seal on the back. Before President Kennedy's bust was put on the half-dollar, Benjamin Franklin was featured. The Liberty Bell was on the back of the Franklin half-dollar. This coin was made of 90 percent silver and is rare today.

Dollar The current $1 coin may look like a gold coin, but it is actually made of a special mixture of copper, zinc, manganese, and nickel. There are two coins in circulation today that represent the gold-colored $1 coin.

The Presidential Gallery of gold $1 coins shows a U.S. president on the front and the Statue of Liberty on the back.

Each presidential coin has edge lettering that includes the U.S. motto, "E Pluribus Unum," Latin for "Out of many, one." That means we come from many states but we are united as one country. Turn the coin on its side to see the edge lettering.

Native American gold $1 coins show the contributions of the tribes and individual American Indians to U.S. history and development. Sacagawea is honored on this coin. A Shoshone Indian, she helped Lewis and Clark explore the West all the way to the Pacific Ocean in 1804.

You will be amazed at how much detail on a coin comes out when you make a rubbing of it. You can see the incredible amount of work that went into designing, casting, and making a coin.

To make a coin rubbing, you will need:

♦ A pencil or colored pencil

♦ Paper

♦ A coin

First, place the paper on top of the coin. Hold the paper firmly, and keep the coin steady.

Using the side of the pencil lead, rub back and forth across the paper where the coin is lying underneath. Continue rubbing until the entire side of the coin is copied on your paper. Be sure to rub both sides of the coin!

Now find out about the pictures on the coin. Who is this on the front, and what image is on the back? What year was it made, and where was it made?

Akela's OK	Date	Den Leader's OK

REQUIREMENT 5 | Play a game or create a game board with your den or family where you can practice adding and subtracting coins.

There are many fun counting games you can play with your den or family. Here is one game you can try:

CHANGE MIXER

Materials

- Posters with the four different coin names and values written on them, one for each player
- Four orange traffic cones (or chairs) set in a large square
- Music (upbeat)

Instructions

1. Give each player a poster.
2. As the leader plays the music, players walk around the outside of the square.
3. When the music stops, the leader will call out an amount that can be made with the coins.
4. Players must quickly join together at one of the four cones with other players and find the total value of the coins in the group. The goal is for the total value shown on the group's signs to be as close to the value called out as possible.
5. Each group must announce its total correctly. The group that is closest wins the round.

Akela's OK	Date	Den Leader's OK

REQUIREMENT 6 | Create a balance scale.

Balance scales have been used since ancient times to compare the weight of objects.

You can compare the weights of different coins using a balance scale. It has a horizontal beam from which two pans, plates, or baskets are suspended. When the weights are equal, the beam and pans will hang evenly. When the weight of one item is heavier than the other, the beam will dip to the heavier side.

When coins were made of precious metals, such as silver and gold, the dollar coin was the unit of money. Other coins weighed a fraction, or a part, of a dollar's weight. Even though today's coins are not made of precious metals, the principle still works. If you use a balance, you will see that four quarters will balance evenly with an Eisenhower dollar coin. Two half-dollar coins will balance one Eisenhower coin, and 10 dimes will balance. The 1-cent and 5-cent coins were not made of silver, so they do not follow the rule.

You can use it for the activity that follows:

To make a balance scale, you will need:

- ◆ Two paper cups
- ◆ String
- ◆ 10-gallon paint stick
- ◆ Tape
- ◆ Binder clip
- ◆ Pen, pencil, or wooden dowel

To make the balance scale:

1. Poke holes in two paper cups, and tie strings to them.

2. Hang the paper cups from opposite ends of a 10-gallon paint stick.

3. You will probably want to tape the strings to the stick to keep them from falling off when the beam tilts.

4. Now attach a binder clip to the middle of the stick, dangle it from your fingers, and work the clip back and forth on the stick until the stick hangs level.

5. Finally, hang the binder clip from the pen, pencil, or dowel. Set the pencil on a table, and hold it in place with a heavy book. Your scale is complete!

A Scout is trustworthy. Remember to return any coins you borrow for activities.

| Akela's OK | Date | Den Leader's OK |

Using your balance scale, try to find different values of coins that might weigh the same. For example, do five pennies equal the weight of a nickel? Which is heavier? How can you make them equal?

Does the weight of two nickels equal the weight of a dime? Place a dime on one side of a balance scale and two nickels on the other. Which is heavier? You might also go with your parent or guardian to a bank to ask for a 50-cent coin and an older Eisenhower $1 coin. Then compare them to the other coins. Does the weight of either coin relate to its value?

You can use your balance scale to do many coin weight investigations.

7 | Akela's OK   Date   Den Leader's OK

I use coins to pay for pencils at the school store. But I never really looked at coins closely before I did this Wolf adventure. Now I look at coins to see when and where they were made and who and what are in the pictures. I also wonder about all of the places they've been used. You never know what you can learn from a coin!

AIR OF THE WOLF

SNAPSHOT OF ADVENTURE

Every day you are surrounded by something that you probably never think about. It's all around you all the time. You need it just like all other living things. It affects the things you do and the games you play. Have you figured out what it is? It's air!

This elective gives you a chance to play with air. This is the air you breathe in and out about 12 to 20 times each minute. It's the air that lets a baseball pitcher throw a curve ball and the air that runs some tools. It's the air that runs windmills to create a clean, green power source. In this adventure, you'll find out how amazing air is! Get ready to try some science investigations, make a paper airplane, and build your own kite!

> NOTE TO AKELA: Make sure your Scout does not have an allergy to latex before using balloons for science demonstrations and experiments.

REQUIREMENT 1A | Conduct an investigation about the weight of air.

When you walk around, do you ever think about the air pushing down on you?

Air may seem like it doesn't have weight or mass—it's just there, wrapped around us like an invisible blanket.

With your den leader or parent or guardian, find out if air has weight by doing an easy science investigation.

Materials

- Two balloons of equal size
- Three pieces of string at least 6 inches long
- Wooden ruler
- Pair of safety glasses
- Small needle or sharp toothpick

Instructions

Put on your safety glasses. Blow up the two balloons until they are equal size, and tie them to the opposite ends of the ruler. Make sure the balloons are placed at the same distance from the ends.

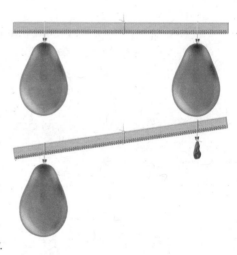

Tie the third string to the middle of the ruler and hang it from the edge of a table or a support rod. Adjust the middle string so the ruler hangs evenly. Now you are ready to begin your investigation.

Carefully pop a hole in one of the balloons with a needle. What happens?

What do the results of this investigation tell you?

The air in the broken balloon has escaped. The compressed air in the full balloon has a greater weight than the air around it. This investigation helps show that air has mass or weight!

1A   **Akela's OK**   **Date**   **Den Leader's OK**

REQUIREMENT 1B | Conduct an investigation about air temperature.

What happens when air gets warmer or cooler? With your den leader or parent or guardian, perform an investigation to find out.

Materials
- Two balloons
- Pan of ice water
- Pan of very warm water (not boiling)

Instructions

Blow up two balloons about halfway.. Place one balloon in the pan of very warm water.

Place the other balloon in a pan of ice water. Wait a few minutes.

Draw a picture of how the balloons changed.

When air is cooled, it tends to contract, or get smaller. When air is heated, it tends to expand, or get bigger.

As the air inside the balloon starts to heat up, it expands. The molecules begin to move faster and farther apart from each other. This is what makes the balloon in the warm water stretch.

There is still the same amount of air inside the balloon. It has just expanded as it heats up! Warm air takes up more space than the same amount of cold air. It also is less dense than the cold air occupying the same space.

1B   Akela's OK   Date   Den Leader's OK

i. **Make a paper airplane and fly it five times. Make a change to its shape to help it fly farther. Try it at least five times.**

ii. **Make a balloon-powered sled or a balloon-powered boat. Test your sled or boat with larger and smaller balloons.**

iii. **Bounce a basketball that doesn't have enough air in it. Then bounce it when it has the right amount of air in it. Do each one 10 times. Describe how the ball bounces differently when the amount of air changes.**

iv. **Roll a tire or ball that doesn't have enough air in it, and then roll it again with the right amount of air. Describe differences in how they move.**

HOW TO MAKE A PAPER AIRPLANE

With a single sheet of 8½-by-11-inch paper, you can make an awesome airplane! Look at the diagrams. Follow the steps, and be sure your creases are precise.

See how far your airplane will fly on five separate flights. Now look at your plane. How could you slightly change it to make it go farther? You can find lots of paper airplane designs in books. With the help of an adult, look online for free paper airplane patterns that you can print out.

1. Fold paper in half.

2. Fold in corners.

3. Fold bent corners to meet in center.

4. Fold in half.

5. Fold down wings.

6. Fly!

HOW TO MAKE A BALLOON-POWERED BOAT

Balloon-powered sleds and boats are fun to make, and they run on air! Here's a balloon-powered boat you can make with help from an adult:

Materials

- Small box (such as a pencil box)
- Sharp knife
- Drinking straw
- Balloon
- Tape
- Small rubber band
- Scissors
- Adhesive putty

Instructions

1. Ask an adult to use the sharp knife to poke a hole in the middle of one end of the container just big enough for your straw to fit through.

2. Cut the straw in half. Attach one end of the straw to the open end of the balloon using tape and wrapping it with the small elastic band. The straw should be attached securely so you can blow up the balloon without air leaking around the sides.

3. Thread your straw through the hole in the boat so the balloon end is on the inside of the boat.

4. Use the putty to secure the straw both inside and outside the boat so it is watertight. Now your boat is ready for the water!

5. Using the straw, blow up the balloon and then kink the straw or put your finger on the end of it so the air doesn't escape.

Put the boat in your bathtub and let go of the straw. Off your boat goes! Try blowing up the balloon a lot and see what happens when you let it go. Then try blowing up the balloon a little bit and letting it go. Tell your parent or guardian or your den leader what you observed.

THAT'S HOW THE BALL BOUNCES!

You will need a hand air pump and a basketball if you choose this requirement. Start with a basketball that isn't completely full of air. Bounce the ball 10 times. Now use the air pump to fill up your basketball with air. Bounce the ball 10 times again.

What did this demonstration teach you about air pressure? The amount of air pressure in a ball has a big effect on how the ball bounces and how high it can bounce. If the ball is properly inflated, the ball will have a higher bounce.

A ball without enough air inside will have a dull bounce and will even come to a dead drop if there is little or no air inside the ball. The amount of air pressure determines how much of the ball's surface will hit the ground.

TO ROLL OR NOT TO ROLL

Air pressure affects the way a tire or a ball handles.

Roll a tire or ball that doesn't have enough air in it. Then roll one that is inflated properly. What did this demonstration show you about air pressure? Tell your parent or guardian or your den leader the differences you noticed between the two.

Akela's OK   Date   Den Leader's OK

Did you know that without air there would be no sounds? Sound travels through the air. Moving air pushes things around, and the things it moves create the sounds we associate with wind.

When the wind is blowing at least a little, what sounds can you hear that are caused by the wind? Does it cause the trees to rustle and the grass to swish in the breeze? Does it cause wind chimes to ring? Can you hear the noise that a bird's wings make when they flap in the wind? If the wind is blowing fast, does it stop you from hearing other things?

The wind may just be "air," but when air moves, it is a mighty force of nature. It can make sounds when it moves over, around, and through things. It can move things. It can turn windmills to make electricity, and farmers can use windmills to pump water for their animals. And if it blows hard enough, such as a tornado or a hurricane, it can even destroy things.

With your den, go outside and record the sounds you hear.

2A   Akela's OK   Date   Den Leader's OK

REQUIREMENT 2B | Create a musical wind instrument, and play it as part of a den band.

Musical wind instruments can be made from many different types of materials. One interesting and easy way to make a wind instrument is to use bottles!

Place different amounts of water in several empty bottles. Blow gently across the openings of each bottle. The more water you put in a bottle, the higher the tone will be. The less water you use in a bottle, the lower the sound will be.

With a little practice, you and your den can make music by playing your instruments together. Talk with your den leader about some instruments you can make.

WOODEN HARMONICA

You may want to make a harmonica. Here is what you need to create one.

Materials
- Two tongue depressors or wide craft sticks
- Scissors
- Paper
- Clear tape
- Three rubber bands (one wide, two skinny)

Instructions
1. Cut two strips of paper the same size as a tongue depressor.

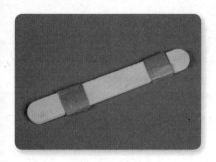

2. Place one tongue depressor on top of the other. Wrap one paper strip around each end of the tongue depressors. Wrap tape around each loop without touching the tongue depressors.

3. Slide off one tongue depressor. Stretch the wide rubber band around the length of the tongue depressor and paper loops.

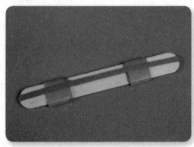

4. Place the second tongue depressor back on top. Wrap one skinny rubber band around each end outside of each paper loop.

5. It's time to make music! Blow air through the middle of your harmonica to play. Slide the paper loops to change the pitch.

Working with an adult, swing something hollow around and above your head. Try swinging a cardboard tube tied to a string. Check your safety circle, and be sure no one is close to you! What happens when you swing the tube faster or slower?

If you cut the tube to make it shorter, what happens to the sound?

Akela's OK	Date	Den Leader's OK

Have you ever flown a kite? Did you know that kites have been used for thousands of years and were invented in China? Boys and girls fly kites for fun. Other people use kites, too, including scientists, weather forecasters, and soldiers.

Here are some basic rules to follow to stay safe when flying a kite:

- ◆ Fly kites away from electrical wires.
- ◆ Fly kites in fair weather. Put them away if a storm approaches.
- ◆ Make kites with paper and wood, never metal—it might attract lightning.
- ◆ Use dry string for kite line.
- ◆ Fly kites in an open field or park, never on a street or anywhere near a railroad line.
- ◆ If a kite gets caught in wires, a treetop, or somewhere else, have your parent or guardian see if it can be retrieved.

3A   **Akela's OK**   **Date**   **Den Leader's OK**

A diamond-shaped kite is easy to fly and will fly even in low wind speeds. Just remember that the larger the paper you use, the better your kite will fly. The heavier the materials you use, the more wind will be needed to get the kite up in the air. Keep your kite lightweight!

Using a paper bag or a newspaper, make a kite.

HOW TO MAKE A DIAMOND-SHAPED NEWSPAPER KITE

Materials
- Two-page spread of newspaper
- Scissors
- Cellophane tape
- String
- Long sticks, bamboo plant rods, or ¼-inch wooden dowels
- Marker

Instructions

1. Draw the shape of a kite on a double-page spread of newspaper. Cut it out.

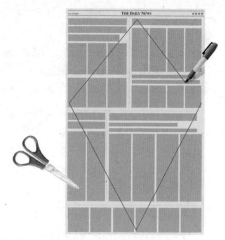

2. Lay two sticks across the diamond-shaped newspaper in the shape of a cross. Tape the two sticks together in the center of the cross or use string to tie the two sticks together in the center tightly.

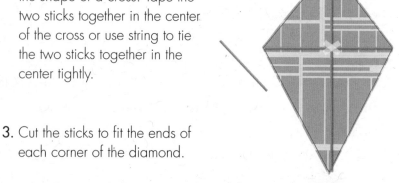

3. Cut the sticks to fit the ends of each corner of the diamond.

4. Make a notch at each of the four corners of the newspaper. Tape all around the outside border of the newspaper to keep the outside edge from tearing in the wind, then tape the wooden cross sticks tightly and securely to the newspaper.

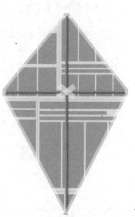

5. Tie a long string onto the middle of the frame and make paper strips for the kite tails. Have fun flying your kite!

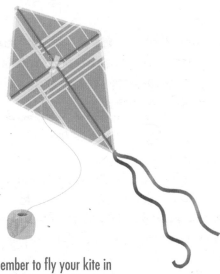

A Scout is obedient. Remember to fly your kite in a safe, open area with help from an adult. Be sure to follow the safety rules!

(3B)

_____   _____
Akela's OK   **Date**   **Den Leader's OK**

I loved making my own kite! But I learned the hard way to stay away from trees when I fly it. Luckily, my uncle had a tall ladder and was able to untangle my kite. Now I only fly it in the open field!

There is nothing like a kite derby, space derby, or raingutter regatta to bring out the creative force of Wolf Scouts! There are lots of books and online sites that have great ideas for building cool kites, airplanes, and boats for den and pack competitions. You can also build one of these just for a fun family project. If you decide to make a kite for this requirement, try a different design than the one you created in requirement 3B. Remember to get permission from an adult before going online.

THE SCIENCE OF AIR

Have you ever wondered how air helps a kite stay up? Or how air helps a sailboat slice through the water?

Wind creates lift. Lift is what happens when wind pushes against an object and carries it up. An object's lift depends on the size of its surface. When the wind carries your kite upward, the wind pushes against the whole surface of the kite to lift it up. That is why your kite floats better than a crumpled piece of paper would with its smaller surface area.

Lift also makes sailboats move through the water. Why don't they fly? It's because their sails point up and down, rather than across like a kite or an airplane wing.

If you like sailing, you might want to become a Sea Scout when you are older. Sea Scouts specialize in water activities such as sailing. You might use what you learned during this adventure in a whole new way!

Talk to your parent or guardian or your den leader about what you've learned about air.

4

Akela's OK   Date   Den Leader's OK

Paper airplanes. Balloon-powered boats. Kites. Musical wind instruments. Science experiments. Turns out air is really something! It has weight and mass. It can power many cool things. You can make music with it, and sound is carried through it. Take a deep breath, Wolf! Get ready to blast off on your next adventure!

CODE OF THE WOLF

SNAPSHOT OF ADVENTURE

Do you ever think about what you want to do when you grow up? Did you know that everyone uses math, either in a job or in daily activities or both? In fact, you use math every day—even if you don't think about it. Have you built something recently? You had to count and measure the pieces. Do you have a favorite team? That team keeps score in games. When you buy something, how do you know that you got the correct change? This adventure helps you to explore how you can use math to have fun.

REQUIREMENT 1 | Do one of the following:

REQUIREMENT 1A | With the members of your den or family, make a game with simple materials that requires math to keep score.

In many games, you use math to keep score.

Here are some ideas for games you can play with your den or your family members:

- ♦ Divide a large piece of cardboard into sections, and mark a number in each section. Try to land paper airplanes on your "aircraft carrier." Add up your points, and the high score wins.

- Mark empty plastic bottles or tin cans with numbers, and roll a ball to see how many you can knock over. Add up your points, and the high score wins.

- Mark a different number in each cell of an egg carton. Mark some with a number to subtract. Drop paper clips or another small object from above the egg carton. Add up the numbers where the paper clips land. After a few rounds, the high score wins.

- Use clothespins or sticks to make a ring toss game. Clamp clothespins around the rim of a bucket or wastebasket. Toss rubber jar rings at the clothespins from 5 feet away. You can give each clothespin a different number if you would like, or just count the number of ringers. Add up your score after a certain length of time or number of rounds.

1A   **Akela's OK**   **Date**   **Den Leader's OK**

This is just like regular "Go Fish," except the goal is to get two cards that add up to 10. Use a regular deck of cards, but take out all the 10s and face cards. Ace counts as 1.

Start with five cards, and put the extra cards face down on the table. If you have a pair of cards that add up to 10, put them down in front of you.

When it's your turn, ask one player for a card that you can add to one of your cards to make 10. If he has the card you asked for, put down the pair, and take one card from the deck. If he doesn't have the card, take one from the deck. Your turn is over when you can make no more pairs that add up to 10. The game ends when you run out of cards.

You might need two decks of cards if there are more than five players.

A Scout is thrifty. If you don't have playing cards, you can make your own deck with index cards.

Akela's OK   **Date**   **Den Leader's OK**

Everyday math is just what it sounds like. You use it every day! For example, you might need to measure something to follow a pattern, or you might need to decide if you have enough money to buy something.

Or you might need to figure out how much silverware you need to set the table for dinner (how many people and how many pieces for each person).

How many plants do you need for a garden if each plant needs a certain space?

What if you want to make a double batch of cookies? How many treats do you need for a den meeting if every boy gets two treats (plus something for your den leader)?

Write down five activities where you have used math at home, at school, or in your den, and then share the activities with your den.

Akela's OK	Date	Den Leader's OK

The rekenrek was designed in Holland. Its name means arithmetic rack. You can make one with some string, 10 red beads, 10 white beads, scissors, and a piece of cardboard. (You can use two different colors if you wish, but use 10 of each.)

1. Cut the cardboard to measure 4 inches by 6 inches.

2. With help from an adult, use the tips of scissors to poke two holes at each of the short ends of the cardboard. The holes should be 1½ inches from the edge of the cardboard and 1 inch apart.

3. Cut two pieces of string 8 inches long. Thread the strings through the holes at one side of the cardboard, and tie knots to hold them in place.

4. Add beads to the strings on the other side of the cardboard. Each row of your rack will contain five beads of one color and five beads of another color in the pattern below. That makes 10 beads on each row of your rack.

5. Thread your strings through the other holes. With help from an adult, tie knots to hold the beads in place.

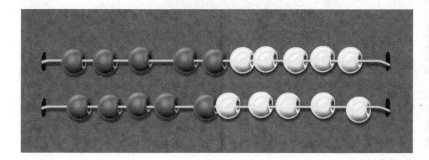

The rekenrek allows you to use different math strategies to come up with the right number or to add and subtract numbers. Start by placing all the beads on the right side of the rack.

As you count the number of beads you need to show a number, push the beads you counted over to the left. Let's say the number you are asked to find is 5. You know that you have five beads of one color and five beads of another color on each line of your rack. You would simply push the first five beads of one color on the first row over to the left. You have just shown the number five on the rekenrek. Or you could count by ones to make five beads on the left.

Now show Akela how you would represent the numbers 4, 6, 9, and 14.

Akela's OK   Date   Den Leader's OK

To make a rain gauge, you can use a plastic soda bottle, colored tape, ruler, scissors, and a pencil or marker.

1. Cut off the top of the bottle where the curved top meets the straight sides.

2. Turn the top upside down and fit it into the base. This will stop the water inside the bottle from evaporating. Drop in several small stones, and fill the base with 1 inch of water. You will measure from this starting point.

3. Add a thin strip of tape around the base at the starting point. Then add a vertical tape strip for measuring rain. Mark ⅛-inch divisions on the measuring tape strip.

4. Place your rain gauge outside, away from any buildings and trees. Record the amount of rain each day for at least a week, and remember to refill or pour out the water down to the lowest division each morning.

1E   **Akela's OK**   **Date**   **Den Leader's OK**

REQUIREMENT 2A | With other members of your den or family, identify three different types of shapes that you see in nature.

Do you ever notice different shapes around you? Sometimes a shape can help you identify something (for example, the shape of a bird's tail).

With members of your den, make a list of all the shapes you can think of. Then take a short hike to see how many different shapes you can find in leaves, flowers, trees, rocks, clouds, and in the grass.

Sometimes, the shapes are made of repeating patterns, such as in the leaves of ferns.

What shape are dandelion flowers? Can you find a leaf that is heart-shaped or an oval? What shape are the nests that birds make? Have you ever looked carefully at a bee's honeycomb? Share the shapes you find in nature with your den leader or a parent or guardian.

2A	Akela's OK · Date	Den Leader's OK

Bridges make it possible to cross over water or other natural barriers, such as canyons. The first bridges were simple stepping-stones placed over a small stream to help people get to the other side. Using the stones as a base, people were able to build a better bridge by placing a toppled tree, a log, or a wooden plank over the stones.

Three common types of bridges are arched bridges, beam bridges and suspension bridges.

The most common shapes used to build bridges are squares, triangles, and cylinders. The triangle is the strongest shape. Triangles are used to make a very strong form called a truss.

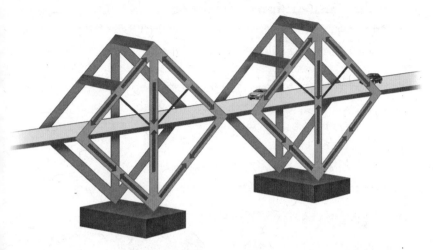

Another strong shape is a cylinder. If you look at your bicycle, you can see that cylinders are used to make the frame strong. They are also used to make piers underneath bridges strong enough to hold a lot of weight. Squares are weaker and can collapse unless the angles are braced. Squares in bridges are braced with triangles to make them stronger.

Take some photos, find some photos, or draw pictures of different bridges. What shapes do you see in the bridges? Are all bridges built the same? Are the shapes different depending on how big the bridge is? Be sure you look at all the shapes, even the smallest parts of the bridge. Identify two shapes used in the bridges you saw. Show your den what you have found, and tell them why you think a certain shape was used.

When artists look at scenes they would like to paint, they may look at them differently than you and I would. They see the pictures in different shapes they can draw. Now you can look at the world around you the way an artist does! What shapes do you see?

Squares and rectangles are easy, and you'll see them all around your house. But you might also see squares in squares (windows) or circles in circles (basketballs through a hoop). Do you see more square, rectangular, or circular clocks? What shape is a bird's beak or the point of your pencil?

Pick a single shape that you like, and write down each time you see it for a week. Share with your den leader or a parent or guardian where you found this shape and how it was used.

Akela's OK   **Date**   **Den Leader's OK**

2C

REQUIREMENT 3A | With your den, find something that comes with many small, colored items in one package. Count the number of items of each color in your package. Keep track of each color. Then:

i. **Draw a graph showing the number of items of each color.**

ii. **Determine what the most common color is.**

iii. **Compare your results to the other boys'.**

iv. **Predict how many items of each color you will find in one more package.**

v. **Decide if your prediction was close.**

Do you ever wonder how predictions are made about the weather? The people who make the predictions have noticed that when one thing happens, another thing is more likely to happen. So if it rained 100 miles away yesterday, it might be more likely to rain where you are today.

Of course, those are just predictions, and they could be wrong. That's why the weather forecasters say there's a chance of rain or snow or sun; they don't guarantee that it will rain or snow or be sunny.

You can make predictions about what is likely and what is unlikely based on your own observations. With your den, select an item to count. You can use colored paper clips, marbles, a small bag of different colored candies, or a snack or cereal with different colored pieces. Count the number of objects of each color in your own package of the item. Then create a graph to show your results and compare your graph to those of the other Wolf Scouts.

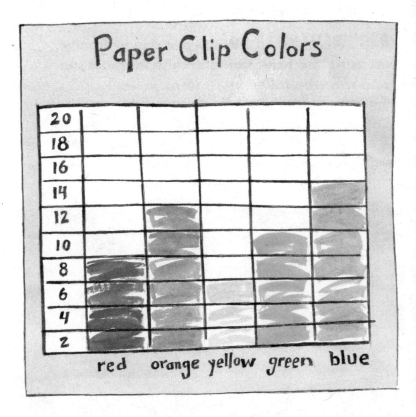

Paper Clip Colors

20					
18					
16					
14					
12					
10					
8					
6					
4					
2					

red   orange   yellow   green   blue

Use the results to make a prediction about how many items of each color you will find in one more package. This is called probability. You can never know exactly what will happen, but you will have a better idea of what to expect based on the results of your investigation.

How close was your prediction? How close did the other boys in your den get to an accurate prediction? Share what you have learned with your den leader or a parent or guardian.

3A   Akela's OK   Date   Den Leader's OK

With your den or your family, mark a starting line and a finish line at least 100 feet apart. Have each person walk from the starting line to the finish line, and count the number of steps he or she takes. Next, measure how tall each person is.

What do you notice? Does everyone take the same number of steps? Who took the most steps? Who took the fewest steps? Do you think it takes more steps or fewer steps if you are taller or shorter?

| 3B | Akela's OK | Date | Den Leader's OK |

Using a graph like the one shown in this picture, show how many shots it takes each person in your den to make five baskets.

With an adult's help, find out what your shooting percentage is by dividing the number of baskets by the number of shots you took.

Remember, a Scout is cheerful. Keep a positive attitude (even if basketball is hard for you), and encourage your Wolf friends. Have fun, and Do Your Best!

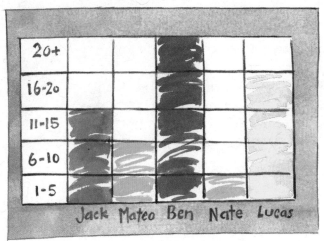

3C   Akela's OK   Date   Den Leader's OK

REQUIREMENT 4A | Use a secret code using numbers to send a message to one of your den members or your den leader. Have that person send a message back to you. Be sure you both use the same code numbers.

What would you do if you had to send a secret message to someone else—a message that no one else should know? You could make up a secret code using math and use a different number for each letter. Then, if someone doesn't know the code, they can't read your message.

People who have to send secret messages do just that. That's another reason to know math—so you can send secret messages or crack someone else's code.

You can find lots of cool codes online (with a parent's permission) and in books. Look for beginner codes that use numbers and then teach the code to one of your den members or your den leader. Send a message in code to the person and see if you can read the message they send back to you!

(4A)   **Akela's OK**   **Date**   **Den Leader's OK**

Besides numbers, shapes can also be used to stand for letters. In the pig pen code, the alphabet is copied into grids. Then, each part of the "pig pen" is substituted for the letter in that part. For the second grid of each type, dots are added.

So, the letter "A" is ⌐ and the letter "W" is ⌄ .

The pig pen code shapes are below:

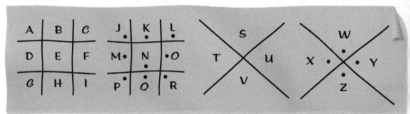

Practice with this message:

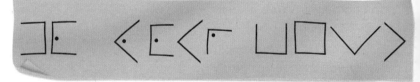

Send a message to another member of your den or your den leader using the pig pen code or another code that changes letters into special shapes.

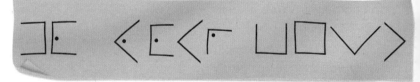

        Akela's OK   Date   Den Leader's OK

A code stick is another fun way to create secret messages. It was used by the Romans in ancient times to send secret messages during times of war. If an enemy warrior stole the secret message, he would not be able to read it.

CODE STICK

Materials
- Piece of paper
- Scissors
- Pencil to wrap the paper around
- Pencil or pen to write with
- Tape

Instructions

1. Cut a long, thin strip of paper about ¼ to ½ inch wide from the side of a sheet of paper.

2. Tape the piece of paper to the top of a pencil. Wrap it tightly around the length of the pencil so the edges of the strip are exactly side by side.

3. Tape the paper strip to the other end of the pencil so the paper strip stays in place when you write on it.

4. Write your secret message down one side of the pencil. Add a few extra letters on other sides.

5. Unwrap the strip of paper from the pencil. The letters should be mixed up and seem random. Pass the secret code to another Wolf.

6. Your Wolf buddy should be ready to wrap the paper strip around a pencil to decode it. The letters will now form the secret message.

See if you can send a message made on a code stick and decode a message sent back to you by a friend!

4C

_____   _____
Akela's OK   **Date**   **Den Leader's OK**

It takes time to figure out a code! It sure is a fun way to send messages once you understand how one works. Did you crack the coded messages, Wolf? Which code did you like the best? Can you write "Wolf Scouts rock" in pig pen code?

COLLECTIONS AND HOBBIES

SNAPSHOT OF ADVENTURE

A hobby is something you enjoy doing in your spare time. Building model airplanes. Model railroading. Reading. Singing. Playing a musical instrument. Leather crafting. Stargazing. Fishing. The list of hobbies is endless.

You can collect just about anything, too. Miniature toy cars. Lunch boxes. Patches. Baseball cards. Stamps. Coins. Postcards. Drawings. You may already have a group of one of your favorite things at home, but you've never called it a collection.

Now it's time to explore what you are interested in, fascinated by, amazed at, and like a lot. Start collecting, Wolf!

REQUIREMENT 1 | Begin a collection of at least 10 items that all have something in common. Label the items and title your collection.

Collecting things is a neat way to celebrate who you are. You may choose to collect something that has special meaning to you or makes you happy. What you collect is done for your own enjoyment, so it can be whatever you like!

Keep in mind that collections don't have to cost a lot. Some people collect rocks, colored bottles, autographs, movie and concert posters, and many other items that are free. Others collect fishing lures, key chains, ceramic dogs, action figures, marbles, and other items that don't cost a lot of money.

Collecting an autograph

People who collect things over time often gain new skills and learn about the objects they enjoy. Collectors enjoy spending free time finding, organizing, and sharing their collections.

Some collectors are generalists. That means they collect a wide range of things— for example, stamps from all over the world. Other collectors are very specific in what they collect, such as only postage stamps from the 1800s.

It may sound funny, but some people collect experiences instead of objects! For example, birders collect the names of the species of birds they have spotted. People who love to travel collect stamps in their passports from visiting foreign countries. Others visit all the state parks or the national parks or all the roller coasters or putt-putt courses they can, and collect bumper stickers or photos. They basically collect memories!

Gather 10 items that follow the same theme. Then, label them and think of a title for your collection. Think about why you enjoy collecting this item and what items you might like to add over time. If you collect trips or experiences with your family, you could label and title the photographs, postcards, or other souvenirs.

Akela's OK **Date** **Den Leader's OK**

Before you bring your collection to share, jot down a few notes to answer the questions below. This will help you remember what you want to tell the den about the items you collect. Tell your den the following things about your collection:

- ♦ What did you collect?
- ♦ Why did you choose that item?
- ♦ Where did you find the items for your collection?
- ♦ How will you add to your collection?

It's fun to share a collection with your den. When you share your interests with your Wolf friends, it gives them a chance to learn more about the person you are and what you like to do. If it's too difficult to bring your actual collection to a den meeting, you can present it another way, such as with photographs.

A Scout is courteous. Remember to listen carefully and be supportive as the other Wolves share their interests and collections, too.

A collection of Scout patches is great to share at a den meeting.

It would be a pretty boring world if everyone had the exact same interests. Have fun celebrating everyone's different interests! Every individual in your den brings something special to your group. What did you learn about the other members of your den when they shared their collections?

2

Akela's OK   **Date**   **Den Leader's OK**

I love going to minor league baseball games with my uncle. I started collecting autographs on baseballs of my favorite minor league players after the games and on fan days. Since I got their autographs, some of those guys have been called up to the big leagues! It's exciting watching them play now that I've met them!

REQUIREMENT 3 | Visit a show or museum that displays different collections or models.

Museums are places where many valuable and interesting collections are displayed for the public. There are antique car museums, train museums, toy museums, art museums, military museums, historical museums, science and space museums, and museums that display the belongings or the historic homes of important people. Some museums tell the story of a town's history. Or they may tell of an important industry, such as mining or ranching.

When you visit a museum near you with your family or den, find out what the museum specializes in collecting. See if you can pick up a brochure that tells more about the museum. If you have questions about the items on display, ask a museum volunteer or staff member. They will be happy to help you understand what the museum is all about.

Share what you learned about the museum and its collection with your den.

3   **Akela's OK**   **Date**   **Den Leader's OK**

The hobby of collecting autographs is known as philography (fi-LOG-ruh-fee). Some people collect autographs because they like the people and any work they may have done. Others collect autographs in the hope that one day the autographs might be worth money. Autographs can be found on almost anything from plain paper to baseballs to musical instruments.

You can create your own simple autograph book using white paper. Make a cover out of construction paper or card stock, decorate it with markers or colored pencils, and turn it into a book by adding a split ring or by stapling the pages together.

Ask for the autographs of your den members, your friends and family, or your coaches and teachers. Show your den leader your autograph book.

Akela's OK   **Date**   **Den Leader's OK**

When you write a letter to a famous person, it doesn't have to be long but it should have a beginning, middle, and end.

Here is how you should set up your letter:

Today's Date

Mr./Mrs./Miss/Dr. and the person's full name
Street Address
City, State, Zip Code

Greeting,

First, tell the person why you are writing a letter. Be polite.

Then, tell why you enjoy what the person does or how you support what they do. Tell a little about yourself, too, and that you are working on your Wolf rank in Cub Scouts.

Finally, say that you would appreciate it if they could send you a photo. Explain that you have enclosed a self-addressed, stamped envelope for them to send you the photo. End by thanking them for their time.

Then sign your letter:

Sincerely,

Your Name
Your Street Address or PO Box
City, State, Zip Code

Your parent, guardian, or den leader may be able to help you find an address for the person you choose to write. Remember to enclose a large, self-addressed, stamped envelope when you send your request.

It may take a couple of months before you receive a reply from a famous person. Good luck!

5

Akela's OK   Date   Den Leader's OK

Your den leader will plan a group game that involves collecting. It might be a scavenger hunt to find 12 pieces of paper with one point of the Scout Law written on each. It might be a tangled web that you have to carefully pass through as you collect items. Or it might be a game where you try to collect clothespins from the back of your fellow Wolves' shirts without losing your clothespins.

Here's a game you can play with your family and friends that uses a collection of objects to test your memory. Get a tray or a large plate, and put 10 to 20 small items on the tray. Place a towel over the tray. Give each player a piece of paper and a pencil. Tell each person playing the game that they have one minute to view the collection. Take the towel off the tray. After one minute, cover the tray again with the towel. Have each player write down all the items that they saw. The player who gets the most items wins.

TAPE WEB

+ Your den leader will create a web that crisscrosses an open space or hallway. (Use painter's tape—the ONLY one that will not stick to walls or lift paint!)

+ If part of the web comes down during the activity, you can help put it back up.

- Stick colored pompoms to the sticky side of the tape.
- When it's time to begin, carefully go through while collecting the pompoms. Don't get caught in the web!

CLOTHESPIN COLLECTION TAG

- This game will get your den moving and paying attention.
- If you need to play indoors due to the weather, use an animal walk, such as a duck or a crab walk, to try and catch each other.

Materials

- Clothespins marked with different colors
- Six or more clothespins in each color
- One color per Wolf

Scouts may only touch clothespins, not grab arms, legs, or clothing.

Instructions

- Begin with all of your clothespins pinned to the back of your shirt.
- Try to collect the clothespins of other Scouts while keeping them from getting yours.

Whatever game your den leader chooses, play fair, be friendly, and Do Your Best, Wolf!

6   **Akela's OK**   **Date**   **Den Leader's OK**

CUBS WHO CARE

SNAPSHOT OF ADVENTURE

In this adventure, you have the opportunity to learn how people with disabilities are able to overcome their challenges and do things others might not believe are possible.

This adventure will help you and your fellow Wolf Scouts understand just how many things people with disabilities are able to do. You will discover some challenges people with disabilities face, and you will have the chance to try facing similar challenges yourself. You can also learn about one amazing person who didn't let a disability stand in the way of a dream.

REQUIREMENT 1 | With the members of your den, visit with a person who has a physical disability.

Most of us never think about how we do certain daily activities, such as walking down the street or watching TV. But many disabled people find new ways to do things in their daily lives and perform the same tasks as others—they just use different tools or steps.

People with physical disabilities are just like you except they have an illness or injury that affects their body's ability to function in some way.

When you meet with a person who has a physical disability, be respectful and polite. If the person is a wheelchair user, try to sit down near them so you can speak to them at eye level. Find out what the person enjoys doing. Ask the person what is difficult for them to do because of their disability.

Are there things that you can do that would be helpful to this person? Are there things that you should not do because they would not be helpful? Always ask people if they need help first, because they may not need as much help as you think!

People with disabilities don't want you to feel sorry for them. They do want you to treat them with respect and kindness, just like you would any person!

If you visit with a person who has a service dog, do not pet the dog without asking first. Service dogs are working animals. They have an important job to do to take care of the person with disabilities. Dogs can open doors, keep people from dangerous situations, and even take out wallets for their owners to pay for items at stores.

Your den may also choose to visit with a person who works with people who have physical disabilities. Talk to that person about how he or she helps people with disabilities. You might learn about things that you can do to help someone you know or someone you will meet.

Akela's OK   **Date**   **Den Leader's OK**

REQUIREMENT 2 | Do four of the following:

REQUIREMENT 2A | With other members of your den, try using a wheelchair or crutches, and reflect on the process.

A single activity can't show you everything about life with a disability. But it can help you understand a little more about the ways a person with a disability is able to do things. In this requirement you will have a chance to try using a wheelchair or crutches to get around. Is it easy or hard? Does it make your hands or arms tired? What would you do if you had to go up the stairs? What if you had to go up or down a hill in a wheelchair? How would you get in and out of a car without help if you couldn't use your legs?

Think about the skills people with physical disabilities develop to be able to use wheelchairs or crutches. Also consider the challenges you encountered and what could be done to overcome them. Talk with your den leader about what you learned.

Akela's OK	Date	Den Leader's OK

2A

"I don't need easy. I just need possible," said Bethany Hamilton. Bethany is a professional surfer who reached her dream of surfing professionally even after losing one arm. People with disabilities who play sports see what's possible and find ways to do what others think they can't.

Did you know that basketball, football, hockey, rugby, soccer, and many other sports have been adapted so people in wheelchairs can play? Archery, handcycling, powerlifting, shooting, swimming, table tennis, and track and field events are just some of the many other sports that people with physical disabilities compete in.

In recent years, many disabled athletes have also started competing in extreme sports, such as kayaking, skateboarding, surfing, and rock climbing.

Organized sports for people with physical disabilities started after World War II. People injured in the war played sports to help them heal.

Today, there are many adaptive sports, which are also called parasports. The Paralympics is a competition for disabled athletes from around the world. A few athletes with disabilities have also competed in events in the Olympic Games, and some are active in professional sports.

Disabled Sports USA helps wounded warriors, children, and adults become active. It has become one of the largest organizations for disabled athletes in America.

Athletes with disabilities have the same desires that able-bodied athletes do. They want to do their best and compete with others. They want to show their independence and will to succeed. Jim Abbott is a former major league baseball pitcher who was born without a right hand. He said that people should focus on what an athlete can do instead of on a disability.

Learn about one sport that has been adapted for people with disabilities. Do you have other ideas for ways that you could change a sport? Share with your den what you learned.

2B

Akela's OK	Date	Den Leader's OK

Our den met with a 16-year-old girl named Marcy who lost the use of her legs in a car accident. She had been very active in gymnastics before the accident. Now she plays wheelchair basketball and loves it! She said playing sports again really helped her get stronger and feel better after the accident.

REQUIREMENT 2C | Learn about "invisible" disabilities. Take part in an activity that helps develop an understanding of invisible disabilities.

Some people have disabilities that others can see, such as disabilities that require a wheelchair. But other disabilities are "invisible," which means that others might not see them.

Invisible disabilities, such as autism or ADHD, can include those that cause people to think or feel things differently than those without the disability. Many children with invisible disabilities are successful in school and activities with some adaptations, or changes, to better fit how they learn.

It can be hard for people to understand what it is like to have an invisible disability. With your den, take part in an activity to help you better understand some types of these disabilities. Some activities will help you understand the spectrum, or range, of autism disorders and how each person with autism is different. After the activity, talk with your den leader about what you learned.

2C Akela's OK Date Den Leader's OK

REQUIREMENT 2D | With your den, try doing three of the following things while wearing gloves or mittens:

  i. **Tying your shoes**
 ii. **Using a fork to pick up food**
iii. **Playing a card game**
 iv. **Playing a video game**
  v. **Playing checkers or another board game**
 vi. **Blowing bubbles**

How important are your hands to you? When you try to do everyday things with gloves or mittens on, you may get a better idea of how much you depend on your hands.

Do the gloves or mittens make it harder to do basic things? Is it just because the gloves or mittens get in the way, or is it because you can't feel what you are trying to do? Would you have to learn how to do things differently if you couldn't use your hands? How would you feel if someone made fun of you because you couldn't do certain things?

People with disabilities find ways to overcome challenges every day. They also must deal with people who do not understand the difficulties they have and say things that are thoughtless.

 A Scout is kind. Remember to treat all people as you would like to be treated. If you see someone with a disability who is having trouble picking up an item or opening a door, ask if you can help!

Akela's OK	Date	Den Leader's OK

You probably count on your eyes to tell you a lot about the world. People who are blind or visually impaired use other senses to give them information about the world around them. They develop an understanding of colors through ideas such as "blue is a cool color, like a glass of water" or "the sun is warm, and yellow and orange are warm colors." They can focus on shape, texture, and size to create an image.

In this requirement, you will draw or paint a picture. Then put on a blindfold and draw or paint the same picture. Get help from one of the members of your den, who may need to guide you to the correct color or to the paper. If you are a helper, think carefully about words and actions that will guide your friend.

When you are finished, think about how it felt different to paint without sight. Did you focus more on the movement of the brush or how you felt as you painted? Did you think differently about the colors you chose? Did your helper guide you clearly? How could you be a better helper if someone you know is visually impaired or blind? Discuss your experience with your den.

| Akela's OK | Date | Den Leader's OK |

How do you use your sense of hearing every day? It is probably an important part of the way you communicate with others. If you couldn't hear someone talking to you, how would you know what the person was saying? Do you think it would be hard to talk if you couldn't hear the sounds you were making? How would you pronounce a word if you had never heard it before?

Many people who are deaf or hard of hearing use American Sign Language (ASL) to communicate. ASL is a visual language (a language you can see) that uses gestures, along with facial expressions and body language, instead of spoken words. It takes practice to learn ASL, but you can start with just a few signs.

Loyal   Friendly   Cheerful   Clean

Learn a simple sentence or four points of the Scout Law in American Sign Language. Teach one of the members of your den the words you learned. Maybe these signs will be just the beginning of learning a new language!

2F

_____   _____
Akela's OK   Date   Den Leader's OK

REQUIREMENT 2G | Learn about someone famous who has or had a disability, and share that person's story with your den.

Many people who aren't famous live with and work to overcome their disabilities every day of their lives. Some have made incredible contributions to society as actors, athletes, world leaders, and in many other professions and fields.

Here are some people you might want to learn about:

Thomas Edison, inventor of the light bulb, the motion picture, audio recording, and more, experienced a hearing loss.

Jean Driscoll won the Boston Marathon wheelchair division eight times and won 12 medals in the Paralympic Games. She was born with spina bifida.

Franklin Roosevelt, the 32nd president of the United States, was paralyzed from the waist down by polio. He was active as a Scout leader and received the Silver Buffalo Award.

Stephen Hawking, a famous scientist and author, was diagnosed with Lou Gehrig's disease (ALS) when he was only 21 years old.

Helen Keller, famous author and lecturer, was deaf and blind.

Erik Weihenmayer didn't let the loss of his vision keep him from mountain climbing. In fact, he climbed Mount Everest!

Share the story of the person you learned about with your den. How did the person's story inspire you?

_____   _____
Akela's OK   Date   Den Leader's OK

REQUIREMENT 2H | Attend an event where people with disabilities are participants or where accommodations for people with disabilities are made a part of the event.

With your den or your family, attend an event where people with disabilities are participants. You may find a local sporting event or one sponsored by Easter Seals or Special Olympics.

AXIS Dance Company performance

You may choose to attend a performance or presentation in which an interpreter uses sign language. Or you may choose a sporting event where deaf athletes compete. You may find an art show or an event that includes the work of people both with and without disabilities. Share what you learned about your experience with the members of your den.

2H

_____   _____   _____
Akela's OK   Date   Den Leader's OK

DIGGING IN THE PAST

SNAPSHOT OF ADVENTURE

Can you imagine birds the size of airplanes flying over your head? How about animals like one of the largest dinosaurs, *Argentinosaurus*—100 tons and 120 feet long—walking through your neighborhood? Can you picture what it would be like to run into a big, bad *T. rex* in the woods? Yikes! Dinosaurs and other giant creatures lived and died out millions of years ago, so thankfully they won't be running by your home anytime soon!

Paleontologists study dinosaur bones and fossils to learn more about their habits, the food they ate, and their size. During this adventure, you will use your Wolf brain to match dinosaurs to their names, and you'll use your Wolf imagination to create your own dinosaur. You'll even use your Wolf taste buds to eat some fossil layers (wow, really?) and your Wolf paws to make fossils and then dig them out!

Millions of years ago, there were many types of dinosaurs and ancient reptiles. There were dinosaur herbivores (plant eaters) and carnivores (meat eaters), plus plesiosaurs (PLEE-see-uh-sawrs) (sea creatures) and pterosaurs (TER-uh-sawrs) (flyers).

Read about some of these creatures below. Then try to match the correct creature to the clues.

You may also play a dinosaur match game with your den or your family members. Give out cards with dinosaur facts on them to half of the people playing the game. Give cards with pictures of the dinosaurs to the other half. Have every player find his match. You can also have an adult cover up the pictures and names for each creature in your handbook. Then, see if you can use the fast facts to guess the names.

HERBIVORES (PLANT EATERS)

Apatosaurus
(uh-PA-tuh-sahr-us)

Fast Facts:

♦ Mistakenly called *Brontosaurus*

♦ Name means "deceptive lizard"

♦ One of the largest land animals, 70 to 90 feet long, 15 feet tall, weighed 30 to 35 tons

♦ Fossils found in Wyoming, Colorado, Oklahoma, and Utah

♦ Featured a long neck, four legs, and a long, whip-like tail

Triceratops
(tri-**SAIR**-uh-tops)

Fast Facts:
- Name means "three-horn face"
- Lived in western North America
- Featured a large bony frill and three horns on its face
- Was a snack for *T. rex*
- Weighed 4 to 6 tons

Ankylosaurus
(**ANG**-ki-lo-sawr-us)

Fast Facts:
- Name means "fused lizard"
- Lived in North America
- Featured a triangular-shaped head, a heavily armored body, and back legs longer than its front legs
- Used its long heavy club tail to break the legs of enemies

Parasaurolophus
(par-uh-**SAWR**-ol-uh-fus)

Fast Facts:
- Name means "near crested lizard"
- Featured a large crest on its head almost 6 feet long
- Fossils found in Canada, New Mexico, and Utah

CARNIVORES (MEAT EATERS)

Tyrannosaurus rex
(tuh-RAN-uh-SAWR-us)

Fast Facts:

+ Name means "tyrant lizard"
+ Lived in forested river valleys in North America
+ Featured huge teeth, strong back legs, short front legs, and powerful tail
+ Was 40 feet long and 15 to 20 feet high
+ Ate other dinosaurs—scientists believe it could eat 500 pounds in a single bite

Spinosaurus
(SPY-nuh-sawr-us)

Fast Facts:

+ Name means "spine lizard"
+ Featured fan-shaped spine on its back, short front legs, and powerful back legs
+ The largest carnivore and may have been longer than *T. rex*
+ Lived on land and in water
+ Ate fish and other small and medium-sized prey

Velociraptor
(veh-loss-ih-RAP-tor)

Fast Facts:

- Name means "speedy thief"
- Hunted in packs
- Could run up to 40 miles per hour in short bursts
- Featured a sharp, curved claw on each foot
- Weighed about 33 pounds
- Ate small animals such as reptiles, amphibians, and smaller, slower dinosaurs

BIRDS

Hesperornithiformes
(hes-pur-or-NITH-uh-formz)

Fast Facts:

- A group of birds with feathers that weren't used for flying but kept them warm
- Lived mostly in water
- Had teeth and ate fish
- Featured webbed feet far back on their bodies for diving
- Fossils found in western North America, Europe, Mongolia, and Kazakhstan
- May have come on land only to nest and lay eggs

Archaeopteryx
(ar-kee-OP-tuh-riks)

Fast Facts:

- Name means "ancient wing"
- Considered to be the oldest known bird
- Lived in southern Germany
- Featured sharp teeth and three fingers with claws on each wing
- Similar in size to a raven
- Ate lizards, frogs, and beetles

PTEROSAURS (FLYERS)

Pteranodon
(tuh-RAN-uh-dawn)

Fast Facts:

- Name means "winged tooth"
- Flying reptile (not a dinosaur)
- Wings spanned 18 feet
- Featured hollow bones
- Fossils found in Kansas and England
- Ate fish and the carcasses of dinosaurs and other animals

Study the traits of each dinosaur or dinosaur relative, and see if you can match the correct creature to the facts in the "Who am I?" box.

A Scout is friendly. Playing games is a great way to make a new friend or have fun with an old one!

Who am I?

1. My protection comes in the form of spines on my body and a long heavy club tail that could be used to break the legs of enemies.

2. I am longer than the *T. rex*; I have a sail on my back, and scientists think I speared fish out of the water.

3. I weigh about 4 tons and have a bony crest on my head.

4. I am only about 12 inches long and have three fingers with claws on each of my wings.

5. I am small and fast. I have sharp claws on my front and hind feet.

6. I have three horns and a bony frill with points on its edges.

7. I use my webbed feet to dive for fish.

8. I am a carnivore with little arms and a big bite.

9. I am a reptile that lived alongside dinosaurs. I was able to fly because I was very light—my hollow bones were filled with air sacs.

10. I am one of the largest land animals. I have a long neck and eat only plants.

_____ *Apatosaurus*

_____ *Triceratops*

_____ *Ankylosaurus*

_____ *Parasaurolophus*

_____ *Tyrannosaurus*

_____ *Velociraptor*

_____ *Spinosaurus*

_____ *Archaeopteryx*

_____ *Pteranodon*

_____ *Hesperornithiformes*

Share with your den other information you might know about dinosaurs.

Akela's OK   **Date**   **Den Leader's OK**

REQUIREMENT 2 | Create an imaginary dinosaur. Share with your den its name, what it eats, and where it lives.

Now you can make up your own dinosaur using your Wolf imagination! A Scout is thrifty, so create one out of recycled objects and common craft items.

Some items you can use include water bottles, laundry soap bottles, soda cans, bottle caps, cereal boxes, container lids, chenille stems, buttons, clay, papier-mâché, cardboard tubes, spools, construction paper, and felt! Remember to ask an adult before you use any of the materials you collect.

Share your dinosaur with your den. Remember, your dinosaur is your own unique creation. Don't forget to make up a name for your dinosaur and tell where it lived and what it ate.

| Akela's OK | Date | Den Leader's OK |

Making your own dinosaur is a cool project. I made an Ethanosaurus with cardboard tubes for legs, plastic juice bottles for a body, and a long head. It had buttons for eyes and sharp teeth made out of toothpicks. My dinosaur lived in the Midwest and ate other dinosaurs. What kind of dinosaur will you make?

Fossils are the remains or impression of a prehistoric organism, or living thing, preserved in earth or rock. Examples of fossils include skeletons, leaf prints, or footprints embedded in the earth's crust.

Fossils and historical artifacts can be found anywhere. The only known *Tyrannosaurus rex* tracks in the world were discovered at Philmont Scout Ranch, the first in 1983 and the second in 2009. Philmont is located in the Rocky Mountains, near Cimarron, New Mexico.

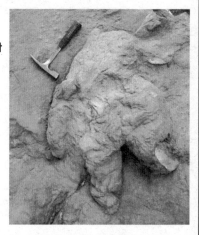

You might have a chance to see it in person if you take a backpacking trip to Philmont when you become a Boy Scout or Venturer.

Some fossils, like the *T. rex* footprint at Philmont Scout Ranch, formed when a dinosaur stepped onto soft ground and left a print. When the ground hardened, a fossil formed. Today, you will have the chance to make your own fossil!

Instead of soft ground, you will use air-dry clay. Roll your clay into a ball in your hand. Pat it down on a paper plate to flatten it out to at least ½ inch thick. It is OK if it looks a little bit lumpy. The ground is lumpy too.

Press a leaf, toy dinosaur, plastic bug, spider, or another object into the clay. You can even use sticks and rocks to form a dinosaur foot! Carefully remove the object. The impression (the dent left behind by your object) is just like the impressions left behind by dinosaurs! Follow the instructions on the package to let your clay harden.

Share the fossil cast you made with your den.

3 **Akela's OK** **Date** **Den Leader's OK**

Paleontologists dig through layers of the ground to carefully uncover bones, rocks, leaf fossils, and other objects that were left behind when the dinosaurs died.

Today, you are going to make your own dino dig! Carefully follow the instructions of your den leader.

Materials for each Scout

- ◆ Disposable aluminum pan
- ◆ Plaster of paris
- ◆ Safety glasses, dust masks
- ◆ Various objects (toy dinosaurs, polished rocks, silk leaves, etc.)

Safety: Be sure to give adults lots of space while they get the mix ready. Adults should wear safety glasses and a mask to keep from breathing in the dust.

Instructions

1. Have an adult mix plaster of paris.
2. Have an adult help you pour enough plaster of paris to cover the bottom of each pan. Place a few objects in the bottom layer.
3. Have an adult help you pour another layer, and place more objects.
4. Repeat until the pan is full.
5. Set the pan aside to dry until the next den meeting.

_____   _____   _____
Akela's OK   Date   Den Leader's OK

REQUIREMENT 5 | Make edible fossil layers. Explain how this snack is a good model for the formation of fossils.

Different types of soil, rock, and weather affected the way fossils formed. Sometimes an object was encased, or completely covered, sometimes it became soft and dissolved, and sometimes rock formed around it. To show fossil

layers, we are going to make a display that you can eat!

Check with your den leader to find out if your den will do this activity as a group. If you would like to try it with your family, follow the directions below.

Materials

- Large, clear plastic cups
- Flavored gelatin
- Animal crackers
- Pudding
- Crushed graham crackers

NOTE TO AKELA: Prepare each cup with an inch of the flavored gelatin in the bottom. Place a few animal crackers in the flavored gelatin before it solidifies. (You want it to absorb moisture.) Prepare a large bowl of pudding and a large bowl of crushed graham crackers.

Instructions

1. Scoop some crushed graham crackers onto the flavored gelatin layer.

2. Place an animal cracker on the layer.

3. Scoop more graham crackers on top, making sure to cover the animal cracker.

4. Scoop pudding onto the graham crackers.

5. Place an animal cracker on the layer.

6. Scoop more pudding.

While eating your fossil layer dessert, notice that some of the animal crackers stay crunchy and some are soft. This is because some of them will absorb moisture from their surrounding layers and some will not. Each of the materials surrounding the animal crackers affects it in a different way.

Now you can see how layers of the earth's crust covered over, surrounded, or even absorbed fossils. The reason that scientists rarely find a complete skeleton of a dinosaur is because some of the bones dissolved over time in the wet conditions of the soil they were in. Who knew fossil layers could be so tasty?

Akela's OK	Date	Den Leader's OK

REQUIREMENT 6 | Be a paleontologist, and dig through the dinosaur digs made by your den. Show and explain the ways a paleontologist works carefully during a dig.

It's time to have a dinosaur dig! Paleontologists use many different types of tools to dig out bones and fossils. Because they do not want to damage anything, they usually use small tools like chisels and paint brushes.

You will be digging through plaster instead of rock, so you can use a large nail, a small hammer, and paint brushes to dig out your objects.

Be careful while you work so you can get the dinosaurs out in one piece!

Safety: For your safety, wear a mask and safety glasses while you work just in case any plaster pieces or dust go flying through the air.

Can you imagine how exciting it must be for a scientist to uncover bones that are millions of years old? Share with your den leader how your dinosaur dig went and what you found.

Akela's OK	Date	Den Leader's OK

FINDING YOUR WAY

SNAPSHOT OF ADVENTURE

The ancient Greeks went on many adventures. Their writings told of faraway lands and treasures. To explain where their adventures took them, they created geography. Geography is the science of the earth's surface. *Ge* means "earth" and *grapho* means "to write."

Maps and compasses are tools that have helped travelers for hundreds of years know if they are headed in the right direction. In this adventure, you will learn to read maps and use one on a hike. You'll also get to make your own map and use a compass on a

scavenger hunt. Just like the ancient Greek explorers, it's time for you to lead the way on another great adventure, Wolf!

REQUIREMENT 1A | Using a map of your city or town, locate where you live.

A map is a drawing or sketch of an area or country. Explorers have used maps since ancient times to travel from one place to another. We use maps every day. You may have used a map to locate a trail you hiked with your den or family. Now it's time to get to know your town better and the area where you live!

You can find a map of your city or town at a public library, the local convention and visitor's bureau, or the chamber of commerce. You can also print out a map of your area from the Internet with your parent's or guardian's permission.

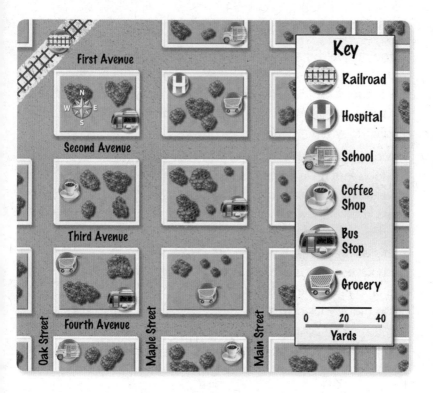

Some online map programs might also allow you to see a satellite image of your street and zoom in on a picture of your home.

You can find the location of your home by typing in your street address with your parent or guardian's help. Your home will not be pictured on a regular city or town map, though.

1A   Akela's OK   Date   Den Leader's OK

Maps have lines, symbols, and colors. A key, or legend, tells you what those symbols and colors mean. Locate the key on the map on page 222. Using the key, locate different symbols on the map. What symbols did you find?

Now make a map of your neighborhood. Include your home, your school, or other locations you choose. Make up your own symbols to show parks, buildings, and bodies of water nearby.

Be sure to mark the streets and landmarks on your map so a friend could easily find the location you selected.

1B

Akela's OK   Date   Den Leader's OK

REQUIREMENT 2 | Pick a nutritious snack, and find where it came from. Locate that area on a map.

People all over the world use maps for transporting goods to different locations. The food we eat is a good that is transported. For example, bananas and pineapples are usually grown in

tropical locations such as Africa, Latin America, and the Caribbean. The bananas or pineapples might need to cross an ocean to get to the United States. Then they are trucked on roads to a grocery store before they get to your home.

How far did your snack have to travel to get to your home? If your snack has a label, check it to find out where the snack was produced. With help from an adult, find a map of the country or state where your snack was produced, made, or grown.

Share with your den what you found out about the snack you chose. Whose snack traveled the farthest?

Akela's OK	Date	Den Leader's OK

I love Honeycrisp apples, so I chose this as my snack. A sign at the store said my apple was grown in Washington state. It sure traveled a long way to get to my home!

224 ▪ Wolf

A compass rose is a figure on a compass, some maps, and nautical charts. It is used to show the four basic geographic directions: north, south, east, and west. This symbol has been used by mapmakers since ancient times.

The term "rose" comes from the figure's compass points, which look a little like the petals of a rose. It was originally used to tell the direction of the winds and was sometimes called a wind rose.

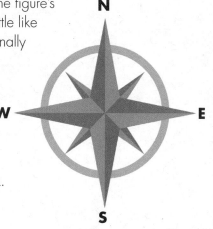

The compass rose is often located in a bottom corner of a map. Reading a compass rose is a lot like reading a clock. You start at the top, which is where north is located.

Here's how to remember the points of a compass rose going clockwise in a circle: **Never Eat Soggy Waffles!**

Never = **North**

Eat = **East**

Soggy = **South**

Waffles = **West**

Look at the map above, and find the compass rose. Now point to a place located in the north on the map. Ask an adult to check—were you right? If you want to keep going, you can name places in the east, south, and west.

3A   **Akela's OK**   **Date**   **Den Leader's OK**

REQUIREMENT 3B | Use a compass to identify which direction is north. Show how to determine which way is south, east, and west.

North, south, east, and west are the points of a compass. A compass can help you figure out what direction is north. Once you know that, you can decide which direction to go to move toward your destination. You can also use a map and compass to figure out how to get from one place to another. Wherever you happen to be on earth, the compass needle will always point north.

Hold a compass flat in your hand. Look down at the needle to see where it is pointing. Turn your body slowly. Keep turning until the compass needle lines up with the north line or "N" on the grid.

Remember the floating needle is magnetized and the red end will always point to magnetic north. You can always figure out the other points of the compass when you stand facing north.

When you are facing north using a compass, east will be on your right, south will be directly behind you, and west will be to your left. If you forget, remember "Never Eat Soggy Waffles" and you'll get right back on track.

Akela's OK   Date   Den Leader's OK

It's time to have some fun using a compass! Your den leader or a parent or guardian will place an object or objects nearby for you to find. Then he or she will give you directions for using the compass to locate them.

First, find north on the compass and line up your body so you are facing north. The adult in charge will give you directions to an object from the position where you are standing.

Using the compass, follow the directions to get to the hidden object. Good luck on your scavenger hunt, Wolf!

4

| Akela's OK | Date | Den Leader's OK |

You've practiced with your map and compass, and now you're ready to try out your skills on a hike. Plan a hike with your den or your family using a park map, a map of your community, or a map you have created.

Be sure to plan the route for your hike so you can follow the directions using your map. Remember to bring along a pack with the Cub Scout Six Essentials and dress for the weather.

When you get to a point on the map that is marked, such as the intersection of two streets or a marked fork in the trail, stop and orient yourself by using the map. Point to the place where you are on the map, and show an adult that you know your exact location.

	Akela's OK	Date	Den Leader's OK

GERMS ALIVE!

SNAPSHOT OF ADVENTURE

In this adventure, you'll get to explore how to keep your body healthy. Why is it important to wash your hands? Why is the slimy mucus in your nose (yep, snot) important to your health? What happens if you sneeze into the air instead of the bend in your elbow? How does keeping your room clean help keep you healthy?

We will explore all of these questions while we journey through the yucky world of germs!

REQUIREMENT 1 | Wash your hands while singing the "germ song."

Have you washed your hands today? You probably get asked that question all the time by your teachers, parents, and other adults. So why is everyone all worked up about keeping your hands clean? Well, it turns out that washing your hands is the best way to keep germs from spreading.

Germs are all around us. They are so tiny you need a microscope to see them, but plants, animals, and people can still get sick from germs.

Four common kinds of germs are bacteria, fungi (FUNG-gahy), viruses, and protozoa (proh-TUH-zoh-uh).

♦ **Bacteria** are tiny germs that live inside and outside your body. The next time you get a sore throat or ear infection, bacteria may be the bad guys.

- **Fungi** live in moist, warm places and can cause itchy rashes and mold.
- **Viruses** get inside your body, spread quickly, and cause colds, flu, chicken pox, and lots of other illnesses.

- **Protozoa** live in water and cause intestinal infections.

You can see why you don't want these germs around! If you want to keep them away, the best place to start is with your hands. Hands are germ magnets. When we touch other people, those germs are passed from hand to hand.

Always wash your hands:
- When they are dirty
- Before you eat and before you handle food or utensils
- After using the bathroom
- After playing outside
- After touching pets or other animals
- Before and after visiting someone who is sick

Here's how to get your Wolf paws perfectly clean:

1. Use warm water to wet your hands.

2. Use soap (any kind is fine).

3. Work the soap into a lather on both sides of your hands. Remember to wash your wrists, between your fingers, and around your fingernails, where many germs hide out.

4. Wash for 10 to 15 seconds (about the time it takes to sing "Happy Birthday" twice), and then rinse off the soap.

Since you're a Wolf Scout now, try singing this song instead to the tune of "Happy Birthday":

No dirty paws for me,
No dirty paws for me,
A Wolf Scout is clean …
No dirty paws for me.

Clean paws keep me strong,
Clean paws keep me strong,
A Wolf Scout is smart …
Clean paws keep me strong!

1

_____   _____
Akela's OK   Date   Den Leader's OK

Now that you have clean hands, let's find out just how far and how quickly germs spread! Play the Germ Magnet game with your den or family.

GERM MAGNET GAME

Instructions

1. Wash your hands, and form a circle with the group.

2. An adult will put a pinch of bright colored glitter into one person's hand in the circle. Have that person shake hands with the next person. Do not touch your face or eyes with glitter on your hands!

3. Pass the handshake around the circle and see how far the "germs" (glitter) go. You can also add a second color to show how different "germs" can build up.

4. Wash your hands after the game. Be sure to clean up all of the glitter with a vacuum cleaner or a broom and dustpan!

What did you learn about how germs are passed by hand contact? Did it help you understand why an important part of the Scout Law we live by is "A Scout is clean"? Share with your den leader what you learned while playing the game.

 A Scout is clean. As Scouts, we keep our minds and bodies fit and clean. We also help keep our homes, communities, and outdoor spaces clean. We do these things out of respect for others, the environment, and ourselves.

NOTE TO AKELA: Make sure that boys don't rub their eyes while they still have glitter on their hands. If your meeting place has glitter restrictions, take the game outside or use washable paint instead of glitter.

2

Akela's OK   Date   Den Leader's OK

Sneezes sound funny, but they are actually a powerful tool your body uses to get rid of dust or other things that are irritating your body.

Sneezing can also spread germs quickly and powerfully. Because a Scout is courteous, always protect the people around you by sneezing into a tissue or the crook of your elbow.

You can conduct a sneeze demonstration to show why you should block a sneeze with your elbow. Because you can't see germs without a microscope, you will use some other items to show what happens when you sneeze.

Materials

- Blanket, old sheet, or tarp with circles drawn on it in the form of a bull's-eye. Each "ring" of the bull's-eye should be 12 inches apart.
- Balloon (check for latex allergies)
- Paper confetti
- Piece of paper to roll into a funnel
- Tape
- Tape measure

Symbols: The bull's-eye represents the air. The balloon is a sneeze. The confetti represents the germs.

Instructions

1. Roll the paper to make a funnel.

2. Insert the small end of the funnel into the balloon.

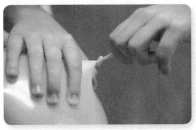

3. Pour a couple of tablespoons of paper confetti into the balloon.

4. Blow up the balloon to its full size and tie it.

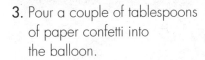

5. Place the blanket with the bull's-eye on the ground.

6. Place the balloon in the center ring of the bull's-eye. Guess how far you think the "sneeze" will spread the germs. Move several feet away from the balloon.

7. On the count of three, yell, "ACHOO!" Pop the balloon.

How far did the confetti spread? Measure the distance the "sneeze" traveled with a tape measure. How did your guess compare to the results? How easy or hard would it be to catch a cold or other illness from a single sneeze?

Remember to clean up after your demonstration and dispose of the confetti and balloon properly.

Akela's OK   Date   Den Leader's OK

Sometimes people call it "snot" or "boogers," but the proper name is "mucus." The slimy stuff inside of your nose has an important job to do. Mucus is a filter. Filters catch objects and make sure that they cannot go any farther.

Mucus catches tiny things in the air that you breathe in through your nose. These could be germs, dust particles, or pollen from plants. No matter what it is that your nose is breathing in, mucus catches it. This is why you should always use a tissue to blow your nose instead of picking it with your fingers.

You are going to make a bag of fake "mucus" and then see how it catches dust. You will also get to see a cool reaction when you mix the ingredients for your fake "mucus" together! A Scout is helpful, obedient, and courteous. Be sure to follow your den leader's or parent's instructions while doing this demonstration.

FAKE MUCUS RECIPE

Materials
- Borax
- Warm water
- White school glue
- Food coloring

- Two plastic containers
- Quart-size zippered storage bag
- Pinch of dirt, flour, glitter, or cocoa
- Paper plate

Container One
- 1/8 cup borax
- 2 cups warm water

Container Two
- 2 teaspoons white glue
- 3 teaspoons warm water

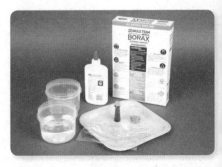

Instructions

1. Dissolve borax into the warm water in container one.

2. Dissolve glue into the warm water in container two.

3. Combine the contents of both containers into a quart-sized zipper storage bag, and add a few drops of yellow or green food coloring.

4. Close the bag, and "squish" the mixtures together to combine them. Continue to knead them until the "slime" forms and all the liquid is absorbed.

After you make your fake mucus, play with it for a few minutes. What does it feel like? How do you think something so slimy could protect your body?

Now put your fake mucus on a paper plate. Place a pinch of dirt, glitter, flour, or cocoa in your hand and gently blow it onto the mucus. Did you notice how it stuck onto the surface? This is how the mucus in your nasal membrane inside your nose filters stuff. Examine the results, and describe what you learned to your parent or guardian or den leader.

Don't forget the final step: wash your hands! This is something we should always do when we handle mucus ... fake or real!

4   **Akela's OK**   **Date**   **Den Leader's OK**

There are different types of mold, and they can grow on many surfaces.

Molds produce and release millions of spores. The spores are small enough to be moved around by air, water, and insects. Some molds also produce toxic agents. Being around mold can make people sick. That is why having a clean home is important to the health of everyone in your family.

With an adult's help, try this mold investigation.

MOLD GROWTH

Materials

- Banana
- Small piece of bread
- Paper plates
- Rubber gloves
- Small piece of cheese
- Sandwich bags

Instructions

1. Place the peeled banana, cheese, and bread in sandwich bags on paper plates.

2. Lightly sprinkle each food with water. Leave a small opening to let some air in.

3. Label the foods with a note that they should not be eaten.

4. Observe the three foods daily.

Which food grew mold faster? Write down your findings for a week. If you can, take pictures to share with your den.

Wear rubber gloves to dispose of the food and paper plates after one week. Have an adult help you clean the area, and wash your hands with soap and water.

What did you learn? Share your findings with your den. Remember to store food properly to stay healthy!

5

Akela's OK   Date   Den Leader's OK

Whoa! I don't have any trouble remembering to wash my hands, sneeze into my elbow, and clean my room now. Do you, Wolf? This adventure really showed me how easily germs spread. I guess the best way to stay healthy is to keep it clean!

Now that you know how bacteria and germs can grow, you can see why it's important to keep your Wolf den (er, bedroom) clean. This healthy habit will give you a healthy habitat.

It can be hard to know where to start when cleaning your room. Make a list of small jobs. Then put the list together in a chart. You can check off each job as you finish it. It feels good to see a completed chart!

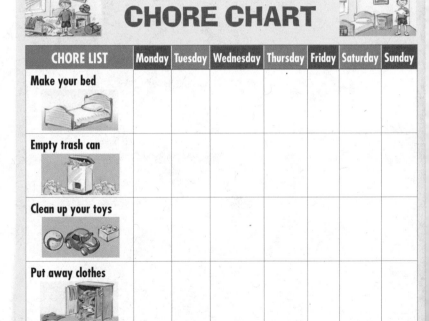

CHORE CHART

CHORE LIST	Monday	Tuesday	Wednesday	Thursday	Friday	Saturday	Sunday
Make your bed							
Empty trash can							
Clean up your toys							
Put away clothes							

6

_____ _____
Akela's OK   Date   Den Leader's OK

GROW SOMETHING

SNAPSHOT OF ADVENTURE

How do plants and vegetables grow? It seems like magic—we prepare the soil, stick a seed in the ground, water it, and before you know it something is growing. Wow! Some plants can even grow in water instead of soil.

Gardening takes commitment and work, but it can be very rewarding. Learning to take care of things is the key. Sun, water, shade, and fertilizer are all things that are very important in helping plants grow. In this adventure, you can try your hand at growing living things and learn more about the plants that are native to your area.

 This elective is also part of the World Conservation Award. (See page 307.)

NOTE TO AKELA: This adventure gives your Wolf an opportunity to learn about the process of plant growth and develop the responsibility needed to care for plants. The activities that follow provide a great chance to spend time gardening with your Wolf.

Many of the plants we see in our daily lives grew from a seed. The seed is put into soil, fertilized, watered, and given a place with some light. Before you know it, a plant is growing. As the plant grows, it may be taken from its container and put into the ground, if it is an outside plant, or put in a bigger container, if it is an inside plant.

Some plants grow quickly, while others take a long time. Radishes grow in about a month, beans grow in about two months, pumpkins and watermelons take about four to five months, but an oak tree can take years just to get as tall as a Wolf.

Choose a seed, and try growing your own plant.

1. Make holes in the bottom of a paper cup so water can drain.

2. Add potting soil.

3. Place the seed in soil as the package recommends.

4. Water the plant, and let it drain in a sink.

5. Place it in a sunny window on a tray.

6. Keep the soil moist, and watch it grow!

How much did your plant grow in 30 days? Take a picture or make a drawing of the plant you grew and share it with your den.

Akela's OK　　　　**Date**　　　**Den Leader's OK**

Different plants require different care. Some plants like a lot of sun, and some like the shade. Some grow where it is cold, and others like the heat. Many like lots of water, but some, like cacti, don't need much water at all. Knowing your growing zone will help you decide what will grow well in your area.

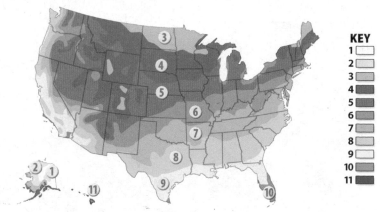

KEY
1
2
3
4
5
6
7
8
9
10
11

Look at the back of seed packages before you buy them to find out if the plants will do well in your growing zone. The seed packets will also give you information about how often to water your plant, what kind of light it needs, and how far apart to plant the seeds.

Do some research at the library or on the Internet (with an adult's permission). Find out what kinds of plants grow best in your zone.

Akela's OK　　　**Date**　　　**Den Leader's OK**

Botanical gardens are large gardens that are open to the public. They are full of plants and flowers, often from far away. Labels tell visitors the botanical (or formal scientific) name of plants and flowers. For example, the botanical name for daisy is *Bellis perennis*. Visitors can learn about the plants or just enjoy looking at them.

A community garden is a piece of public or private land gardened by a group of local people. People might share the work or have separate small plots of land to garden. Community gardens usually produce vegetables and fruits.

There are many botanical and community gardens throughout the United States.

Think about some things you would like to find out before you visit one.

- ◆ Which plants are easy to grow?
- ◆ How much light and water do different plants need?
- ◆ What other things do plants need to grow?

NOTE: If you do not have a botanical or community garden in your area, you can visit a nursery or local garden club.

Akela's OK   Date   Den Leader's OK

REQUIREMENT 4 | Make a terrarium.

When you create a terrarium, you build your own little world of plants inside a clear container. Terrariums look like aquariums, but they are made for plants instead of fish.

Terrariums are a good way to watch plants grow. They are made out of clear glass or clear plastic containers. You can make an open terrarium without a lid on it or a closed terrarium with a lid.

Choose a few plants for your terrarium that do well in the same kind of environment. You can plant small ferns, begonias, ivy, and moss together because they like the soil to be moist. You can use a lid with these plants because they like humid air. If you see a lot of water droplets forming inside the container though, you should remove the lid for a while and then replace it.

You can also plant cactus and other succulents together because they need very little water. Use an open container because these plants need lots of air.

Materials

Small plants of different colors, textures, and shapes (Look for plants that don't grow too big for the container to hold.)

Optional materials include moss, decorative rocks, tiny pine cones, shells, or small figures such as an animal or tiny garden gnome

Clear glass or clear plastic container (clean)

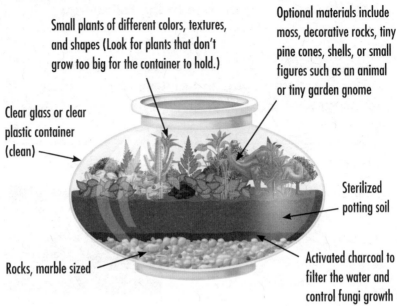

Sterilized potting soil

Rocks, marble sized

Activated charcoal to filter the water and control fungi growth

Follow the picture to build your terrarium from the bottom up.

1. Place a 1-inch layer of rocks on the bottom.

2. Add a ½-inch layer of charcoal.

3. Fill the container half full of potting soil.

4. Plant small plants; leave space between them so they have room to grow.

5. Optional: Add decorative rocks, shells, or a small figure.

6. Water the plants a little, but not too much.

7. Place the terrarium in indirect light.

Share the terrarium you made with your den.

| 4 | Akela's OK | Date | Den Leader's OK |

REQUIREMENT 5A | Using a seed tray, grow a garden inside your home. Keep a journal of its progress for 30 days. Share the results with your den.

It's easy to start your garden inside your home in a seed tray.

Materials

- ♦ Plastic tray
- ♦ Potting soil
- ♦ Vegetable seeds

Instructions

1. Fill the tray half full with potting soil, and dampen.

2. Make lines across the soil for seed rows.

3. Place seeds in the rows. Leave space as directed.

4. Cover the seeds with a thin layer of soil.

5. Leave the tray where it is warm and light.

6. Keep the soil damp, and watch your indoor garden grow.

Every few days, take a close look at your seed tray and write down any changes you see in your journal. Before long, you should see seedlings pushing up out of the soil and leaves starting to grow. If you have an outdoor garden space and the weather is warm enough, you can plant the vegetables outside once they have grown to about 3 or 4 inches in height.

5A   Akela's OK   Date   Den Leader's OK

A plant does not always have to be in soil to grow. There are certain types of plants that will grow in water. Putting your plant in water will allow you to see the roots that will go deep in the ground once the plant is planted.

Materials

- Clear glass jar with a wide opening
- Wooden toothpicks
- Sweet potato

Instructions

1. Check that the sweet potato will fit in the jar with space around it. Push three or four toothpicks into the sweet potato to make a circle around the middle.

2. Rest the toothpicks on top of the jar. The upper half of the potato should be above the opening.

3. Fill the jar with enough water to cover the bottom half of the potato.

4. Place the jar in a window with plenty of sunlight.

5. Check the water regularly to be sure it covers half of the potato.

It will take two or three weeks to see any change in the potato. Then you will start to see roots growing from the potato's buds. The roots will reach down into the water. You will also see green leaves starting to grow from the top.

You can leave your potato in the jar, water it, and watch the vines grow longer. Or you can replant it to a hanging basket in good soil when the leaves and roots have really started to grow. If you plant it in the ground in good soil, the sweet potato may spread and produce sweet potatoes that can be eaten!

Share the journal you kept of your plant's growth with your den.

5B

_____ _____ _____

Akela's OK **Date** **Den Leader's OK**

When my veggies got too big for the trays, I moved them outside and planted them. In just a few months, we were eating fresh salads! The veggies tasted really good because they had just been picked. How did your garden grow, Wolf?

HOMETOWN
HEROES

SNAPSHOT OF ADVENTURE

There are heroes all around us. A hero is someone we admire for being brave or good. Many heroes don't even think they are heroes. A hero takes care of people, helps others, and lives by beliefs like those in the Scout Oath and Scout Law. In fact, you will find many heroes who are part of Scouting. In this adventure, you will have the chance to learn about, talk to, and celebrate heroes in your hometown!

NOTE TO AKELA: This adventure gives your Wolf an opportunity to learn about people with heroic qualities. It also provides a great opportunity to discuss and discover how your Wolf feels about helping others and living the Scout Oath and Scout Law.

There are many reasons a person is called a hero. Being brave, helping someone in need, and putting others first are some reasons people are called heroes. Police, firefighters, service members, doctors, and nurses are also thought of as heroes. Ordinary people can be heroes, too—even kids like you!

A Scout is brave. One way to become brave is to learn about others who have done brave things.

Think about someone you believe is a hero. This could be someone you know or someone you have learned about. You could visit the library, or, with your parent's or guardian's permission, go online to learn more about the person. Find out what he or she did that was brave, caring, or special to help others. Share what you learn with your parent or guardian and your den.

Akela's OK	Date	Den Leader's OK

Police officers and firefighters are trained to protect us from harm. They must be ready to risk their own lives to help others. Doctors and nurses are trained to take care of us, no matter how badly injured or sick we are. Service members are trained to protect our country from harm and to rescue their fellow soldiers in danger. There are many other places in your town where heroes work every day.

With your den or family, visit a place where people help others. Some choices are:

- EMT station
- Police or fire station
- School
- Veterans Affairs office
- Public health office
- Another community agency

Before you visit, write down some questions you would like to ask. Be sure to thank the person or people you meet for their service to your community and for taking the time to meet with you. Share what you learn with your den.

_____   _____
Akela's OK   **Date**   **Den Leader's OK**

REQUIREMENT 3 | With the help of a family member, interview one of your heroes, and share what you learn with your den. Tell why you think this person is a hero.

When you select a hometown hero to interview, think about people in your school, family, and community.

Here are some questions you might want to ask him or her.
1. What is your favorite part of your job?

2. What was your scariest or most difficult day on the job?

3. What keeps you coming back day after day?

4. How did you prepare for this job?

5. Who is your hero?

6. How does it make you feel to be able to help or protect others?

7. What qualities does a person need to do your job?

Be sure to end the interview by shaking hands and thanking your hero for serving the community. Share what you learned about your hometown hero with your den.

Akela's OK	Date	Den Leader's OK

Many service members might be away from home for the first time. A package from home with the things they love is a great way to lift their spirits and let them know that the people in their hometown care about them.

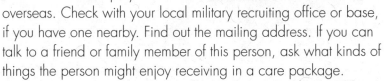

With your den leader's help, identify a service member who is deployed overseas. Check with your local military recruiting office or base, if you have one nearby. Find out the mailing address. If you can talk to a friend or family member of this person, ask what kinds of things the person might enjoy receiving in a care package.

Working with your den or your family, put together the care package. It might include favorite snacks, a magazine or good book, music, socks, sunscreen, candy, a game, and other fun things. Ask your den leader what you are allowed to send.

Write a note to include with your package, thanking the person for serving our country. Tell a little bit about yourself, and share some news from your hometown. Tell them you would really enjoy meeting them when they return from active duty and to stay safe.

| Akela's OK | Date | Den Leader's OK |

Animals can be heroes too. Police dogs are trained to help police. These dogs can locate drugs, search for people who are lost, and help take criminals into custody.

Other service dogs and animals are trained to help people who are disabled, blind, or elderly, or have mental or physical limitations.

Hearing dogs, or signal dogs, can be the ears of people who are hearing impaired or deaf. They can alert their owners to doorbells, oven timers, people calling their names, and other everyday sounds. They use a paw touch or nose bump to get their owners' attention. When they hear a fire alarm, these dogs are trained to take their owners outside.

Guide dogs help people who are blind or visually impaired. They help people get around town on foot and with many other tasks.

Other service dogs help people with physical disabilities. They are trained to open doors, pull clothes off hangers, pick up dropped items, bring medications and the telephone, and do things that their owners cannot do on their own.

Remember, service animals are working. Ask permission before approaching a service animal.

Horses, cats, and other animals are also trained as therapy animals to bring cheer and provide stress relief to sick children, elderly people, and people with disabilities.

Find out about animals in your community that help people. You will be surprised how many animal heroes are living around you!

5

Akela's OK	Date	Den Leader's OK

It is an honor to recognize those who are heroes. You and your den can find many opportunities to do just that.

Think about participating in an annual parade on Veterans Day or placing flags on service members' graves for Memorial Day. You may be able to take part in or help plan a neighborhood picnic to honor someone special in your community. Or you can help plan a homecoming celebration for someone from your town who has served overseas.

Work closely with your den to choose an event or to plan a way to honor someone. How did you feel honoring that person? Why are you proud to have him or her in your community? What have you learned about being a hero while you worked on this adventure?

Akela's OK	**Date**	**Den Leader's OK**

My friend Tom's dad is in the armed forces. Last year Tom's dad helped us organize a pancake breakfast for service members at his base. My pack and other people helped out, and we made a gazillion pancakes. I was proud to thank them for everything they do to keep us safe. And they loved the pancakes!

MOTOR AWAY

SNAPSHOT OF ADVENTURE

There are many ways to make things go—electricity, fuel, and batteries, to name a few. Do you know that *you* have the power to make a boat sail in the water, make a spool car move forward, or make an airplane fly across the room?

Propulsion is what gives an object (such as a plane, car, or boat) the power to move. You will learn different ways to make and propel vehicles. Think about how the shapes of cars, boats, and planes affect the distance they can go. In this adventure, you will explore how you can use the air in your lungs, the strength of your Wolf paws, and the power of your imagination to make things go!

REQUIREMENT 1A | Create and fly three different types of paper airplanes. Before launching them, record which one you believe will travel the farthest and what property of the plane leads you to make that prediction.

Paper airplanes are light. This helps them fly through the air when you use the power in your muscles to propel them. But a real airplane is heavy. How does anything that big stay in the air?

Airplanes need to have lift to fly. Scientists explain lift with an idea called Bernoulli's (bur-NOO-leez) principle. As planes travel through the air, air travels over the wings. The shape of the wings makes the air travel faster over the top than beneath them. This creates higher pressure beneath the wings than above them. The pressure difference causes the wing to push upward, creating lift. The faster the plane moves through the air, the more air is forced under and over the wings, creating more lift.

Bernoulli's Principle

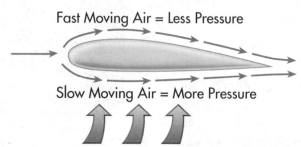

Fast Moving Air = Less Pressure

Slow Moving Air = More Pressure

To help understand how the principle works, try this with a sheet of paper:

Another way to help a plane fly is to add elevators. (No, not elevators you can ride on!) Elevators are the flaps at the back of the plane that give it lift or cause it to dive.

Now it's time to make your own paper airplane. Choose one of the following plane designs or try your own design. See how different wing shapes change how the planes fly. Make careful, crisp folds to help your planes fly farther and faster.

You can also add details like elevators. To make elevators, cut 1-inch flaps on each wing. Flip them up to make the plane rise. Flip them down to make the plane drop. Try flipping one elevator up to make the plane turn.

Elevator Flaps

ARROW

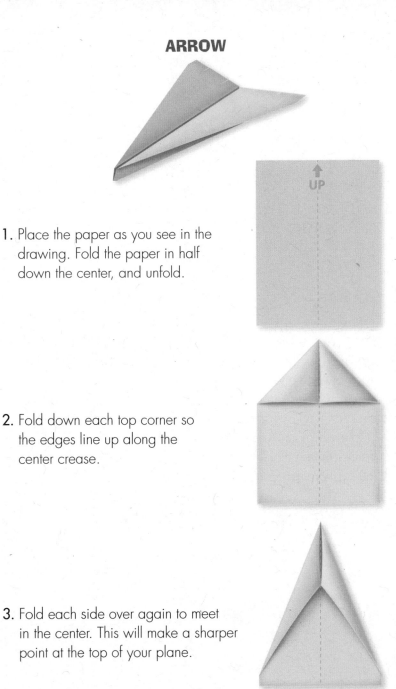

1. Place the paper as you see in the drawing. Fold the paper in half down the center, and unfold.

2. Fold down each top corner so the edges line up along the center crease.

3. Fold each side over again to meet in the center. This will make a sharper point at the top of your plane.

4. Flip the paper over.

5. Fold the plane in half down the center. You should see the folds on the outside.

6. Starting 1 inch from the the tip, make a crease straight to the back of the plane to create the wing. Repeat on the other side to match. Then lift the wings up so they are flat. You might choose to cut two slits about 1 inch apart on each wing to create elevators. Angle the wings so you see a "V" from the front. This can make the plane more stable. Get ready for takeoff, Wolf!

Elevator Flaps

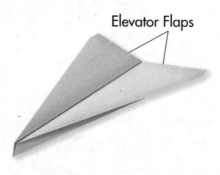

DELTA

1. Place the paper as you see in the drawing. Fold the paper in half down the center, and unfold. Now fold it in half in the other direction, and unfold. You should have four boxes from the creases.

1.

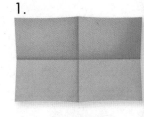

2. Fold down the top corners so they meet in the center.

2.

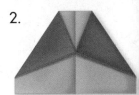

3. Fold the top edge down to the center.

4. Fold each top corner to the center along the crease running from top to bottom.

5. Fold the left side over the right side so the folds are hidden.

3.

6. About 1 inch from the nose, start to fold down the wings in a straight line to the back of the plane. When both wings have been folded, lift them up to a slight "V" shape.

4.

5.

6.

DART

1. Place the paper as you see in the drawing. Fold the paper in half down the center, and unfold.

2. Fold down each top corner so the edges line up along the center crease.

3. Again, fold the outside edges to the center crease. This will create a sharper point at the top.

4. 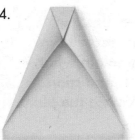   **5.**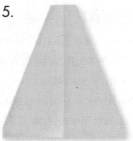

4. Fold down the point to the edge of the folded flaps.

5. Flip over your paper so the flat side is up.

6. Fold the plane in half.

6.

7. On one side, fold the tip in half at a slight angle. Make a crease to the back of the plane to create the wing. Repeat on the other side. You can add elevators, if you choose.

You are ready to fly! Before you fly your three planes, guess how far each will go. Measure the distance after each first flight and see how close you came to guessing the distance each plane traveled. Share the results with your den.

7.

_____ Akela's OK   **Date**   **Den Leader's OK**

Make a paper airplane catapult. Before launching a plane, record how far you believe it will travel and explain what information you used to make this prediction. After you make your prediction, launch the plane and measure how far it flies.

Have you ever seen pictures of a fighter jet being launched from an aircraft carrier? Because the ship has a short runway, the flight deck crew hooks the jet to a catapult to fling it into the sky.

In the last requirement, you used your arm to thrust the plane forward. This time, a rubber band will propel the plane. Stretching the rubber band backward creates tension.

Because the material in a rubber band will return to its original size when you let go of it, the tension throws the plane forward as the rubber band shrinks. Listen carefully as your den leader or parent or guardian explains the safety rules for you to follow. Stay safe and have fun, Wolf!

> **NOTE TO AKELA:** To make sure your Wolf stays safe while launching items, consider putting a tape line around your "launch area." Use a countdown as a signal to the boys to leave the launch area. Make sure the rubber bands are in good shape.

PAPER AIRPLANE CATAPULT

Materials
- Paper airplane
- Hole punch or scissors
- Rubber band
- Tape measure
- Pencil

Instructions

1. Using one of the paper airplanes you made for Requirement 1A, punch a hole through the underside of the paper airplane. If you are using scissors, have an adult carefully make a hole for you.

2. Use a pencil to thread the rubber band through the hole.

3. Tie the rubber band to the plane as shown.

4. Write down how far you think your plane will travel.

5. Find an open space outside. Never point the plane toward a person! Make sure no one is near your launch area so everyone stays safe and has fun.

6. Loop the rubber band over your thumb. Hold the back underside of the plane firmly. Pull back on the plane to stretch the rubber band. Let go of the plane, and watch it soar!

7. Measure the distance the plane traveled with a tape measure.

My prediction: _____

Actual distance: _____

How far did your plane go? Share your findings with your den.

1B

Akela's OK   **Date**   **Den Leader's OK**

There are many kinds of boats. Some have motors. Some have sails. Some carry cargo. Some carry people. Some go fast, and some go slow. The shape of the boat depends on the job it is supposed to do.

BUOYANCY

The buoyancy of an object measures whether it will float in water. Why is it that some objects float and some sink? You probably know from playing with objects in the water that a block of metal will sink and a piece of wood will float.

You also know that many large boats are made out of metal and they float. What makes this happen?

Whatever the boat is made from, it takes up space in the water. The amount of space it takes up is called displacement. If the amount of water the boat displaces weighs the same as the boat, the boat will float. You can try this by making a boat out of aluminum foil. Try different shapes to see which one holds the most cargo. You can use 1-cent coins to see what shape holds the most.

WHAT MAKES BOATS MOVE

Some boats use sails, and other boats use motors. Still others are moved through the water by using paddles.

The hull, or body, of the boat is important, too. Boats made to handle rough water have V-shaped hulls. Boats made for calm water or to carry heavy loads often have flat hulls.

BUILD A BOAT

You might want to look around your house for things to use to build your boats. Use the facts about boats to help you make a model boat that works like a real boat. For different types of boats, you could use a water bottle, a milk carton cut in half lengthwise, an egg carton, corks stuck together with toothpicks or wrapped with rubber bands, or part of a pool noodle.

Your boat could be long or short, round or streamlined. For a round boat, you could recycle a yogurt container or a sour cream tub. For the mast you could use a straw, a craft stick, or a stick from outside. For the sail, you could use a piece of paper or a piece of craft foam. Each choice you make will affect the way your boat moves.

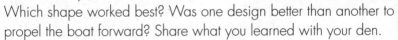

Move your boats in the water by blowing air on the sails. While sailing your boats, notice how they are similar and how they are different. Talk about what you learned with your den.

What kind of boats did you make? How did they move in the water?
Which shape worked best? Was one design better than another to propel the boat forward? Share what you learned with your den.

> **NOTE TO AKELA:** For safety reasons, choose a small wading pool or other shallow container of water for floating the boats. Do not leave Scouts alone near the water. Place an adult in charge of that area. Do not use a swimming pool, pond, river, or lake to float the boats.

2

Akela's OK   Date   Den Leader's OK

There are many ways to make a car that moves. A balloon-propelled car or spool car requires the power in you to create the momentum. Momentum is the force and strength of something when it moves. When you blow up the balloon or wind the rubber band and let go, the car moves. Here are a couple of ideas you might try.

BALLOON CAR

Materials

- Pint milk carton, cleaned
- Balloon
- Two straws
- Four spools
- Skewers

Instructions

1. Cut one straw to create two pieces the same size as the side of the carton.

2. Slide one skewer through each straw. Slide a spool on each end, then tape the ends to hold the spools in place.

3. Lay the straws across the carton, and tape them in place. Check that the skewers can turn freely.

4. Slide the other straw into the balloon. Tape the end of the balloon to the straw so no air will escape.

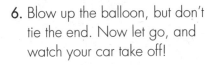

5. Turn the carton over. Tape the straw with the balloon to the top of the balloon car.

6. Blow up the balloon, but don't tie the end. Now let go, and watch your car take off!

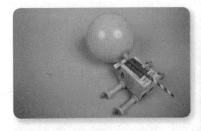

SPOOL CAR

Materials
- ◆ Spool
- ◆ Rubber bands
- ◆ Two washers
- ◆ Two paper clips
- ◆ Tape
- ◆ Pencil

Instructions

1. Unfold one paper clip. Use it to push the rubber band through the hole in the spool until the rubber band goes all the way through.

2. Put a paper clip through one end of the rubber band, and tape it to the end of the spool.

3. On the other end of the spool, thread two washers through the end of the rubber band. Then stick a pencil through the loop in the rubber band.

4. Hold the spool in one hand while you turn the pencil around and around in a clockwise direction to wind the rubber band tightly.

5. Put the spool on a flat surface and watch it go!

Test your balloon car or spool car on a carpeted surface, a smooth floor, a sidewalk, and the grass. How does your car work on each of these surfaces? What happens when you blow up the balloon only part of the way? Does the car go as far? What happens when you don't wind the rubber band tightly on the spool car? How far did your car travel? Share what you learned with your den.

3   **Akela's OK**   **Date**   **Den Leader's OK**

There isn't one "right" way to make your car. You might want to try different materials or a different design to see what works best. That's the fun part of building stuff!

If your car doesn't move the way you want, think about the problem. Then make some changes, and try again. Good luck, Wolf!

PAWS OF SKILL

SNAPSHOT OF ADVENTURE

Sports and active games are a great way to have fun and be healthy. You can also learn a lot about life playing them. Sports teach you to work with a team, help others, and follow rules. You can use the Scout Oath and Scout Law as guides when you are playing games and sports. In this adventure, you'll be challenged to exercise, play a team sport with your den, run an obstacle course, and show how to be a good sport. Time to move your powerful paws, Wolf!

What does it mean to be physically fit? Physically fit people have healthy hearts, lungs, and muscles they have developed from exercise. They don't get tired easily. They have a healthy weight. They are flexible so they move easily. Because they eat the right foods and exercise regularly, their bodies can fight off sickness better.

Eating a low-fat diet of vegetables, fruits, protein, and grains and limiting sugary foods is also important to help your body have energy to burn and build strong muscles.

Running, riding a bike, swimming, walking, and playing team sports are just a few ways you can stay fit. You should try to be active at least three times a week for 30 minutes each time. The trick is to do something you like and just get moving!

Now think about what you eat, how often you exercise, and the types of exercises you do. What can you do to be more fit? Share ideas with your den about what you can do to stay in shape.

Some exercises help build muscles.

Some exercises help improve your heart and lungs.

Akela's OK   Date   Den Leader's OK

Stretching can warm you up before exercising or cool you down after.

A 10-minute warm-up will get your heart ready for activity. It will also loosen your muscles and help keep you from being injured.

After you exercise, spend about 5–10 minutes cooling down. These slow exercises help slow down your heart rate, keep your muscles from getting sore, and improve your flexibility.

Here are some warm-up and cool-down stretches you can try:

Take time to warm up and cool down each time you exercise. Demonstrate the warm-up and cool-down exercises you do to Akela or your den leader.

| Akela's OK | Date | Den Leader's OK |

You can't exercise just one time to become fit. When you practice your fitness skills many times, you will get better at doing them. Over time, you will be able to do more of each skill.

Choose two physical fitness skills, and practice them every day. Skills can include jumping jacks, sit-ups, pull-ups, or running in place.

1. Jumping jacks

2. Sit-ups

3. Pull-ups

4. Running in place

See if you are able to do more of each skill after practicing for two weeks. Remember to warm up before you begin and cool down when you are done.

Write down the skills you performed in the chart below. Write the number of each skill you were able to do at the start, after one week, and after two weeks.

Skill	Start	After Week 1	After Week 2
1. _____	_____	_____	_____
2. _____	_____	_____	_____
3. _____	_____	_____	_____
4. _____	_____	_____	_____

Share what skills you did and how you improved with your parent or guardian or your den leader.

3

Akela's OK   **Date**   **Den Leader's OK**

When you play a sport by yourself, you can practice and improve on your own.

When you are part of a team, you need to work with others to get better. One player can't do everything. Each member helps the team in some way.

Make a list of team sports with your family or den. Think of ways a team works together to be successful. Choose one team sport to play for 30 minutes.

We chose: _____

In Scouting, you have already learned a lot about the importance of teamwork. Remember to support your teammates and play by the rules. Also be sure to treat coaches, other players, and referees with respect.

How did your team work together? How did you help your team?

Akela's OK	**Date**	**Den Leader's OK**

REQUIREMENT 5 | With your den, talk about sportsmanship and what it means to be a good sport while playing a game or a sport. Share with your den how you were a good sport or demonstrated good sportsmanship in requirement 4.

It is important to be a good sport while playing sports and games.

Here are some tips for showing good sportsmanship:

1. Play by the rules.

2. Be courteous to everyone.

3. Cheer for good plays.

4. Try your best.

5. Play to have fun.

6. Shake hands after the game.

A Scout is helpful. You make a difference to your team when you are helpful—both on and off the field.

Share with your den how you practiced good sportsmanship when you played a team sport.

_____   _____
Akela's OK   **Date**   **Den Leader's OK**

REQUIREMENT 6 | Visit a sporting event with your family or your den. Look for ways the team works together. Share your visit with your den.

With your family or den, attend a sporting event. Your den can agree on a sport that is in season near you. The players might be in high school or college, or they might be professional players.

See if you can find out some information about the players and the team before you go. It also helps to understand the rules of the game before you watch a sporting event. It's more fun to watch if you know something about the team and how the game is played.

Tell your den about the ways you saw team members work together and how they showed sportsmanship.

6

_____   _____
Akela's OK   **Date**   **Den Leader's OK**

REQUIREMENT 7 | With your den, develop an obstacle course that involves five different movements. Run the course two times and see if your time improves.

Obstacle courses combine many activities. You get to move in different ways and try new skills. Like other sports activities, you can improve your time on an obstacle course with practice.

Work with your den to choose and create five activities. Here are some ideas:

- Crawling under a table or bench
- Jumping over soft pool noodles
- Tossing a ball or beanbag into a bucket
- Running through a sprinkler
- Weaving through cones
- Walking backward for 10 steps
- Balancing as you run along a snaky garden hose

What part of the course was easy for you? Was any part of the course difficult? Were you able to improve your time? Just as you pitched in to help your den build the course, be sure to help break it down afterward.

Akela's OK   **Date**   **Den Leader's OK**

My den worked together to make a really fun obstacle course. On my first try I couldn't jump over the pool noodle. But my den cheered me on like crazy, and on my second try I made it over! That felt pretty cool. How did you and your team do, Wolf?

SPIRIT OF
THE WATER

H2O

SNAPSHOT OF ADVENTURE

Can you guess the answer to this riddle?

I can be a solid, liquid, or gas. I am two-thirds of your brain, and I can also be two-thirds of a tree. I existed during the days when dinosaurs were wandering around the earth and I have not changed. What am I?

If you guessed water, you are right!

Water is an important force in our lives. It can be as gentle as a spring rain or as powerful as a hurricane. All living things need water to live, but we use water for more than just survival. We use it for fun, too! In this adventure, you will learn how to conserve water, how to keep yourself safe in the water, how to become a better swimmer, and how to have a great time splashing around.

REQUIREMENT 1 | Demonstrate how the water in your community can become polluted.

All communities need a way to get clean drinking water. Water comes from lakes, rivers, or wells tapped into an underground water source called an aquifer. The water is filtered, and then it travels through a maze of pipes to your faucet. Where does the drinking water in your community come from?

Water pollution is when water becomes spoiled by chemicals, waste, trash, or other particles. Polluted water can become harmful to people, fish, and animals that need fresh water to survive.

Did you know that the water molecules that were on the earth when dinosaurs lived are the same water molecules that are around today? When we pollute water, that same water stays in the environment.

A lot of water pollution comes from human activities.

Here are some of the sources of water pollution:

SOME CAUSES OF WATER POLLUTION

Hazardous chemicals

Soaps and detergents

Trash and litter

Oil and other chemicals

Air pollution from cars

Pesticides and fertilizers

 A Scout is loyal. Taking care of the water in your community is a way to show loyalty.

WATER POLLUTION DEMONSTRATION

This activity will show you how quickly pollution can spread through groundwater.

Materials
- Clear glass loaf pan or baking pan
- Powdered drink mix (red or purple in color)
- Sand
- Spray bottle filled with water
- Book or small block of wood

Instructions

Make a small pile of powdered drink mix in one end of the clear glass pan. Sprinkle sand over the rest of the pan. Place the end of the pan with the powdered drink mix on top of the book or wood block so the pan is tilted. Using the spray bottle of water, wet the sand. (Make sure it's really wet.) Let it sit for a few minutes, and then wet it again. Carefully lift up the pan and look underneath it. What is happening?

The water is carrying the powdered drink mix through the loaf pan. Pollution can travel a long distance and can damage drinking water miles from where it starts!

Think about how water is used in your community and how it might be polluted. Share what you learned about water pollution in your community with your den.

Akela's OK   Date   Den Leader's OK

Water is important to our planet. It is up to all of us to help conserve it, not waste it. What can you do to save water in your home?

First, think about the ways your family uses water. Include how you do the following activities:
- Brushing teeth
- Bathing
- Washing dishes
- Watering the grass or plants
- Cooking food

Look at your family's current water bill. How many gallons of water per month do you use? Find a gallon-size container to help you picture the amounts.

Now, think about how you could use less water doing everyday tasks. Here are some ideas:

1. Turn off the tap while you brush your teeth. Turn it back on to rinse your mouth. You could save up to eight gallons of water a day and 200 gallons each month! That's enough to fill a large fish tank!

2. If you wash dishes by hand, do not let the water run. You can save up to 200 gallons of water a month.

3. Take five-minute showers. Short showers use much less water than filling a bathtub.

4. Turn off the faucet completely each time you use it. Fix faucet leaks. A little drip can waste hundreds of gallons of water.

5. Water your yard early in the morning or in the evening. That keeps the water from evaporating quickly in the heat of the day.

6. Wash your car or bike with a bucket of water. Do not let a hose run the whole time.

Share with your den one way you will save water at home. Make saving water a good habit!

2

_____   _____   _____
Akela's OK   **Date**   **Den Leader's OK**

Swimming is a fun way to help you become fit and healthy. Swimming helps you develop stronger muscles. Each kick and arm stroke pushes you through the water. Water is about 12 times as dense, or thick, as air. That means you must work harder to move in the water.

Your lungs and heart also become stronger when you swim. Swimming helps your heart provide better blood flow throughout your body.

For people who are injured or disabled, swimming is often a safe way to exercise. Your body does not need to support all of its weight in the water, so swimming puts less stress on an injury.

Talk to your den leader about why swimming is good exercise.

3 | Akela's OK | Date | Den Leader's OK

REQUIREMENT 4 | Explain the safety rules that you need to follow before participating in swimming or boating.

Let's get ready to swim! Start by learning how to stay safe around the water.

When you were a Tiger, you learned the **SCOUT** water safety chant. Use it when you go swimming or boating.

S is Someone's watching. Never swim alone.

C is Check the rules. Know where you can roam.

O is Only buddies should go from the shore.

U is know what "U" can do. Don't do any more.

T is Tell a grown-up if someone is in need.

SCOUT shows safety. Now you take the lead!

A buddy is your partner in the water. Always stay with your buddy! Your buddy will swim with you and will be there in case you need something. The buddy system makes swimming safer.

When you swim with your den, there will be a buddy check. Swimmers should stop where they are, join and raise hands, and wait quietly with their buddies. Leaders will count pairs to make sure everyone is safe and with their buddy.

Demonstrate the buddy check and repeat the **SCOUT** safety chant for your den leader or Akela.

adult supervision

life jacket

You also need to learn how to stay safe when you go boating.

Here is what you need to remember:

1. Only go boating with adult supervision.

2. Always wear a life jacket when you go boating.

3. A balanced boat will help keep the boat from tipping over.

When you go boating, always follow the safe boating rules explained by your leader or lifeguard. Explain what you've learned about safe boating to your den leader.

Akela's OK   Date   Den Leader's OK

Sometimes people in the water need help. Maybe they are just a little tired and need a pull. Or they might be in a canoe that tipped over. Maybe they slipped off a dock.

Here is how you can be prepared to help:

First, call for help from a lifeguard or another adult. If no adult is there, you can take action.

The first thing you can do is REACH from the shore. Do not go in the water. Find an object to use to reach for the person who needs help. It could be a pole, pool noodle, or a branch. Lie down before you reach so you don't get pulled into the water. Make sure you talk to the person and say, "Here, grab this!" Stay calm.

If reaching does not work, call again for a lifeguard or an adult to help. Always remember that you are not expected to do more than you can do. Keep yourself safe.

Akela's OK	Date	Den Leader's OK

Now it's time to try some new skills at the pool. The first thing to practice is blowing bubbles out of your nose in the water. This skill will keep the water from going up your nose when you jump in.

Before you make a splash, you need to know how to safely jump feet first into water. The best way to jump is with your arms forward and legs slightly apart, one in front of the other.

Lifeguards, scuba divers, and Scouts like you enter the water this way to avoid dangers beneath the water.

Once you are in the water, do your best to swim at least 25 feet. Swimming is a lot like other sports. When you practice it, you get better and faster.

One stroke you can use is the front crawl. To do the front crawl, lie on your stomach in the water. Kick your feet behind you and paddle forward with your arms. If you are unsure how to do a front crawl, ask an adult for help.

6   **Akela's OK**   **Date**   **Den Leader's OK**

When my Wolf den went to the pool, my best friend, Tom, and I decided we would do every swimming stroke we knew. We swam the crawl, the breaststroke, and the backstroke. We tried to do the butterfly stroke, but we both looked like whales crashing into the water. We need a lot more practice to get better at that stroke!

SPECIAL AWARDS YOU CAN EARN

The following awards can be earned while you are a Cub Scout. Check with your pack leaders or go to **Scouting.org** (with a parent's or guardian's permission) to learn more.

Conservation Good Turn Award

The Conservation Good Turn is an award packs may earn by partnering with a conservation or environmental organization to choose and carry out a Good Turn in their home communities.

Outdoor Activity Award

Tiger, Wolf, Bear, and Webelos Scouts have the opportunity to earn the Cub Scout Outdoor Activity Award. Scouts may earn the award in each of the program years as long as the requirements are completed again each year. Cub Scouts complete specific requirements for each rank, including a number of different outdoor activities.

National Summertime Pack Award

The National Summertime Pack Award encourages packs to be active when school is out for the summer. Youth and adult pack members can earn the award by taking part in one activity per month in June, July, and August.

Outdoor Ethics Awareness Award
Outdoor Ethics Action Award

Cub Scouts who are interested in learning more about outdoor ethics and Leave No Trace may earn the Outdoor Ethics Awareness Award. The Outdoor Ethics Action Award asks Scouts to use their new knowledge to take steps to improve their outdoor skills.

STEM/Nova Awards

The Nova awards for Cub Scouts are for Wolf, Bear, and Webelos Scouts who are interested in learning more about science, technology, engineering, and mathematics. These awards may not be earned by Tiger Scouts.

For their first Nova awards, Scouts have the opportunity to earn the Nova award patch, followed by three more π pin-on devices. The patch and the three devices represent each of the four STEM topics. The Supernova awards have more challenging requirements and recognize more in-depth, advanced achievement in STEM-related activities.

World Conservation Award

The World Conservation Award for Cub Scouts provides an opportunity for individual Wolf, Bear, and Webelos Scouts to "think globally" and "act locally" to preserve and improve our environment. This program is designed to make youth members aware that all nations are closely related through natural resources, and that we are interdependent with our world environment.

Requirements for this award must be completed *in addition to* any similar requirements completed for rank. This award may not be earned by Tigers.

Bobcat Trail

Your name _____

Fill in seven tracks to earn the Bobcat badge.

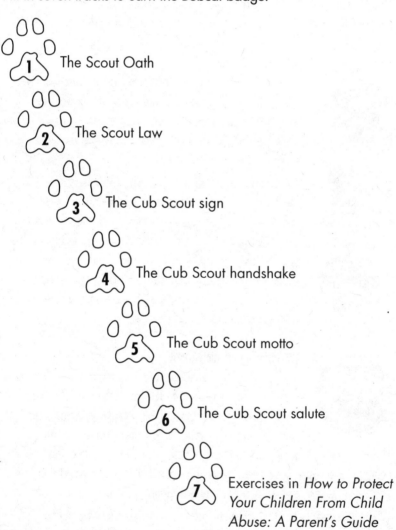

1. The Scout Oath

2. The Scout Law

3. The Cub Scout sign

4. The Cub Scout handshake

5. The Cub Scout motto

6. The Cub Scout salute

7. Exercises in *How to Protect Your Children From Child Abuse: A Parent's Guide*

Wolf Adventure Tracking

1. Complete each of the following Wolf required adventures with your den or family:

Required Adventures

Call of the Wild
(1) (2) (3) (4) (5A) (5B) (5C) (6)
(7A) (7B) (7C)

Council Fire
(1) (2) (3A) (3B) (4A) (4B) (5) (6A)
(6B) (6C)

Duty to God Footsteps
(1A) (1B) (2A)   Do TWO of these.   (2B) (2C) (2D)

Howling at the Moon
(1) (2) (3) (4)

Paws on the Path
(1) (2) (3) (4) (5) (6) (7) (8)

Running With the Pack
(1) (2) (3) (4) (5) (6)

2. Complete one Wolf elective adventure of your den or family's choosing.

My elective adventure: _____

3. With your parent or guardian, complete the exercises in the pamphlet *How to Protect Your Children From Child Abuse: A Parent's Guide*, and earn the Cyber Chip award for your age.*

*See full requirements on page 28.

Elective Adventures

Adventures in Coins ① ② ③ ④ ⑤ ⑥ ⑦

Air of the Wolf 1A 1B 1C 2A 2B 2C 3A
3B 4

Code of the Wolf

Do TWO of these. 1A 1B 1C 1D 1E

Do ONE of these. 2A 2B 2C

Do ONE of these. 3A 3B 3C

Do ONE of these. 4A 4B 4C

Collections and Hobbies ① ② ③ ④ ⑤ ⑥

Cubs Who Care ① Do FOUR of these. 2A 2B 2C 2D 2E
2F 2G 2H

Digging in the Past ① ② ③ ④ ⑤ ⑥

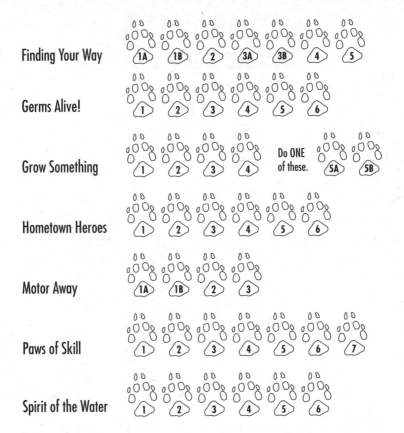

Finding Your Way
1A 1B 2 3A 3B 4 5

Germs Alive!
1 2 3 4 5 6

Grow Something
1 2 3 4 Do ONE of these. 5A 5B

Hometown Heroes
1 2 3 4 5 6

Motor Away
1A 1B 2 3

Paws of Skill
1 2 3 4 5 6 7

Spirit of the Water
1 2 3 4 5 6

GET SET FOR THE BEAR ADVENTURES!

Wow! Think about all of the amazing things you've done, Wolf! Your den has explored the outdoors, helped your community, and learned a bunch of new skills. (And you had a ton of fun doing it!) So what's next? Well, if you have finished the second grade or are now 9 years old, you can begin to work on the Bear adventures! Keep on Cub Scouting!

CREDITS

Acknowledgments

The Boy Scouts of America gratefully acknowledges the contributions of the many Cub Scouts, Scouters, subject experts, and staff throughout the nation for their help in preparing the *Wolf Handbook*.

Photo/Illustration Credits

Illustration

ChooseMyPlate.gov—page 122

Jeff Ebbeler—pages 41, 45, 54, 66, 69, 73, 77, 116, 117, 120, 121, 130, 135, 152, 159, 160, 171, 173, 174, 182, 184, 189, 193, 197, 199, 223, 228, 246, 247, 261, 286, 298, 299, 301, and 304–305 (*swimming*)

Chris Folea—pages i, 16, 27, 31, 38, 49, 51, 61, 65, 69, 73, 79, 81, 91, 93, 95, 104, 109, 111, 116, 123, 139, 155, 157, 177, 182, 192, 195, 213, 224, 242, 255, 265, 281, 293, 305, and 311 (*bottom*)

Aleksey Ivanov—pages 86–89 (all), 232–233 (*all*), 236, 243, 289, 290, and 296

John McDearmon—page 12 and inside back cover

Grant Miehm—page 257

Rob Schuster—pages 36, 37, 44, 53, 57, 64, 84, 108–109, 142, 143, 145, 153, 154, 155, 163, 164, 168, 175, 176, 222, 248, 251, and 268–273 (*all*)

Photography

Courtesy of AXIS Dance Company. Dancers: Joel Brown & Sebastian Grubb. In choreography by Amy Seiwert. Photo by David DeSilva. 2012—page 203

BSA—pages 3, 4, 9, 25, 50, 68, 70 (*bottom*), 140, and 300

Tom Copeland—page 186

Courtesy of Jean Driscoll—page 201 (*middle*)

Caroline Finnegan—pages 67, 137, 138, 241, 253–254, 297

Elias Goldensky, Library of Congress Prints and Photographs Division—page 201 (*bottom*)

Library of Congress, Prints and Photographs Division—pages 55 (top and bottom left), 76, 201 (*top*)

Whitman Studio, Library of Congress Prints and Photographs Division—page 202 (*middle*)

Courtesy of Spencer G. Lucas, Ph.D.—page 214

Ryan Mitchell—pages 22 and 256

Roger Morgan—pages 6, 72, 86, 179, and 292

NASA.gov—page 202 (*top*)

Brian Payne—pages 244, 266, 276 (top), and 284 (right)

Randy Piland—pages 10, 24 (both), 30, 32, 42, 46, 47, 59, 80, 90, 92, 96, 110, 112, 113, 114, 115, 118 (bottom), 119, 124, 151, 156–157, 158, 161, 162, 172, 181, 187, 188, 190, 196, 198, 215 (top), 216, 218, 220, 221, 227, 229, 231, 245, 248, 252, 259, 265, and 284 (left)

Michael Roytek—pages 1, 2, 8, 11, 12, 14–15, 17, 18, 23, 33 (all), 35, 48, 52, 60, 74, 78, 83, 94, 97, 98, 99, 101, 102, 105, 106, 118 (top), 146, 149, 150, 165, 178, 200, 204, 215 (bottom), 230, 234, 235, 237, 238, 239, 240, 260, 264, 267, 268, 275, 276 (bottom), 277, 278–280, 282, 285, 302, and 303

Courtesy of Shutterstock.com—pages 13 (©Panachai Cherdchucheep), 39 (chipmunk, ©Wildphoto3; butterfly, ©Mrsirap), 40 (turtle, ©Paul Reeves Photography; bird, ©Steve Byland), 50 (flag, ©Naypong), 55 (present Salt Lake City, ©Andrew Zarivny), 56 (Wichita, KS 1880, ©Stocksnapper), 58 (spiral wire, ©kenate), 62 (hands and towel, ©Oleg Kozlov), 63 (water bottles, ©lucadp; recycling paper, ©Ritimages), 67 (pots, ©Jillian Cane), 70 (adobe house, ©almondd), 71 (cemetery, ©Delmas Lehman), 81 (stars, ©Nicemonkey), 82 (stars, ©Ronnie Howard), 100 (stop sign, ©tkemot), 106 (hawk, ©Robert L. Kohthenbeutel), 107 (deer, ©David Byron Keener), 125 (stamp, ©Ethan Daniels), 128 (minting machine, ©s spopov), 129 (Denver mint mark, ©Henryk Sadura), 132–133 (background coins, ©STILLFX), 147 (basketball, ©Aaron Amat; pump, ©Deslife), 148 (windmills, ©Beata Becia), 166 (silo, ©Vaclav Volrab; bees, ©Studio Smart), 167 (arched bridge, ©Israel Hervas Bengochea) 168 (beamed bridge, ©Toa55; suspension bridge, ©f11photo), 169 (geometric buildings, ©Wolfgang Zwanzger), 180, (shell collection, ©Anna Biancoloto; stamp collection ©Denemmanuel), 183 (toy cars, ©Caruso Christian), 185 (background for letters, ©Oksana Boguslavska), 194 (both, ©mezzotintl), 195 (bike, ©mezzontintl), 205 (dinosaurs, ©Elenarts), 206 (Apatosaurus, ©Catmando), 207 (Triceratops, ©3Dalia; Anklyosaurus, ©ArchieMKDesign; Parasaurophus, ©Jean Michel Gerard), 208 (T-rex, ©leonello calvetti; Spinosaurus, ©Valentyna Chukhlyebova), 209 (Velociraptor, ©3Dalia), 210 (Archaeopteryx, ©leonello calvetti; Pteranodon, ©Catmando), 211 (background for fossils, ©Jane Rix), 212 (dinosaurs realistic, ©Computer Earth), 217 (sandstone, ©alysta; crackers, ©Danny Smythe), 219 (fossil, ©stockphoto mania), 224 (fruit market, ©elexeinez), 225 (compass rose, ©Zmiter), 226 (map with compass rose, ©deer boy), 226 (compass rose, ©Zmiter), 245 (planting supplies, ©Dzioebk), 249 (urban garden, ©Jane Rix), 250, (grass/terrarium, ©Africa Studio; cacti/terrarium/cacti, ©Armei Studio), 254 (sweet potato vine, ©Sony Ho), 255 (avocado tree, ©KPG Payless), 257 (parade, ©Dale A Stork), 258, (father and son, sonya etchison), 262 (service dog, ©Jeroen van den Broek; rescue dog, ©Jim Parkin), 263 (therapy dog, ©Monkey Business Images), 283 (hockey player, ©Lorraine Swanson), 288 (boy running to base, ©Steve Bower), 291 (football players, ©Michael Chamberlin), 294 (boys on tubes, ©Christophe Rolland), and 314 (©Denise LeBlanc)

N. Tamura/CC-BY-SA-3.0—page 209 (Hespernornithiformes)

Courtesy of the U.S. Mint—pages 126 (all), 127 (all), 128 (coins with mint marks), 129 (coins), 131 (all), 132 (all isolated coins), 133 (all isolated coins), 134 (United States Golden Dollar Coin obverse featuring Sacagawea © 1999 United States Mint. All Rights Reserved. Used with permission.), 134 (all other coin images)

Courtesy of Erik Weihenmayer/Touch the Top—page 202 (bottom)

Notes

Notes

Notes

Notes

THE OUTDOOR CODE

As an American, I will do my best to—

♦ Be clean in my outdoor manners,
♦ Be careful with fire,
♦ Be considerate in the outdoors, and
♦ Be conservation minded.

LEAVE NO TRACE*
PRINCIPLES FOR KIDS

Know Before You Go
Choose the Right Path
Trash Your Trash
Leave What You Find
Be Careful With Fire
Respect Wildlife
Be Kind to Other Visitors

*The member-driven Leave No Trace Center for Outdoor Ethics teaches people how to enjoy the outdoors responsibly. This copyrighted information has been reprinted with permission from the Leave No Trace Center for Outdoor Ethics: www.LNT.org.